The Legends of Carter's Grove and Other Mysteries:
A Selection of Essays from the Journal of Colonial Williamsburg

By Alan Simpson

The Colonial Williamsburg Foundation
Williamsburg, Virginia

Library of Congress Cataloging-in-Publication Data

Simpson, Alan, 1912–
       The legends of Carter's Grove and other mysteries: a selection
   of essays from *Colonial Williamsburg*, the journal of the
   Colonial Williamsburg Foundation / by Alan Simpson
           p.   cm.
       Articles published between 1986 and 1993.
       ISBN 0-87935-097-0
       1. Carter's Grove (Va.)   2. Burwell family.   I. Title.
   F234.C35S56   1993
   975.5' 425—dc20   93–29524
                                                    CIP

Printed in the United States of America

For Mary

Whom I first met as a fellow graduate student in the Bodleian Library, Oxford, and have now enjoyed as companion, wife, mother, editor, and co-author for over 60 years.

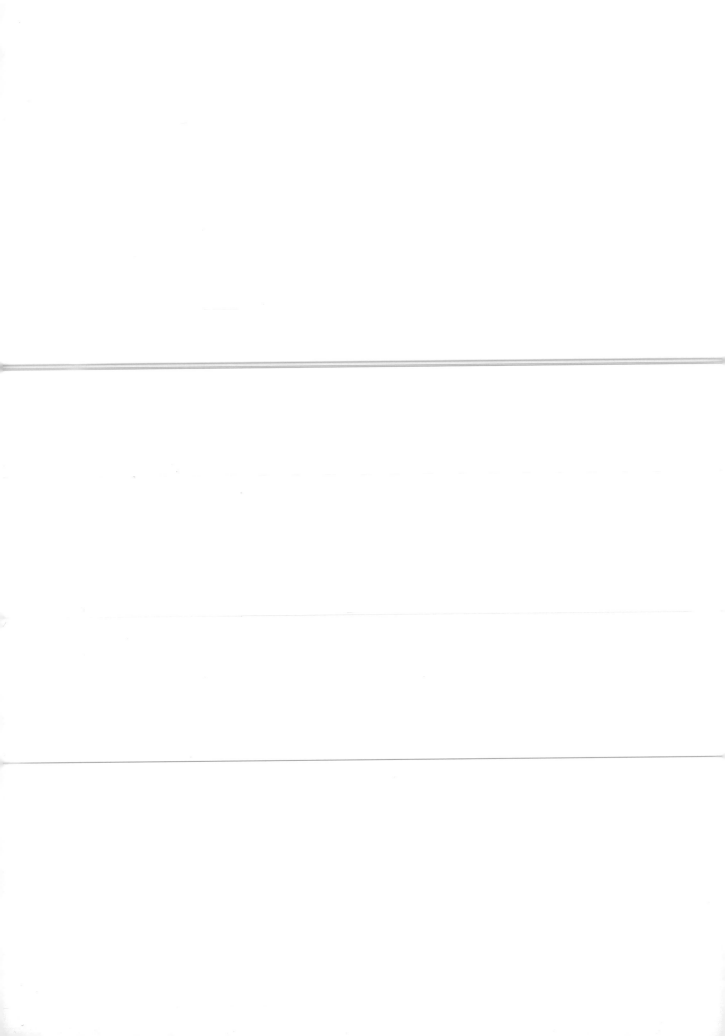

CONTENTS

PREFACE

There is an element of detective scholarship in all historical research, but it was only as I approached retirement that I found myself absorbed by several mysteries in the colonial history of New England and Virginia and decided I would try to solve them.

Typical puzzles in New England, where Little Compton was to be my year-round residence, involved various episodes in King Philip's War. How had our village hero, Colonel Benjamin Church, whose journals Mary and I had just edited, acquitted himself in the eyes of both races, red as well as white? Why was our Proprietor's Map of Indian lands such a muddle? Which of the 50 villages in England called Compton, whether Long or Little or whatever, had anything to do with the adoption of our name? This was useful training for stiffer tests to come.

Williamsburg had been a sort of second home for over 20 years because of my connections with the Institute of Early American History and Culture and the Colonial Williamsburg Foundation. Old maps have always intrigued me, so I fell under the spell of the anonymous Frenchman's Map, the so-called "Bible of the Restoration" because of its picture of streets and buildings in the old capital during the Yorktown Campaign (1781). We believe we left the secret of its identity more than half-solved.

Equally intriguing to an English-born historian who remembered his schooldays in ancient grammar schools followed by five years in Oxford colleges, was the elusiveness of the planter's schooldays in England. A case in point was Robert "King" Carter. A crusty complaint in his middle age about what he was shelling out to educate his own sons over there, compared with what "old Mr. Bailey" had charged to board him for six years, was almost all we knew about his education.

In time we would pinpoint the home of Arthur Bailey and his son Arthur, tobacco factors, near Stepney Green in London's east end, on a map of the parish drawn in 1701 by Joel Gascoyne, a top surveyor; offer a plausible conjecture that Carter's own school was the Coopers School in Ratcliffe; and demonstrate beyond doubt that his eldest son John Carter of Shirley was educated in a private academy in Stepney by a distinguished scholar-teacher whose picture we found on a print.

All seven stories in this selection, which postdated the two we just mentioned, were drawn from the history of Virginia, and published in *Colonial Williamsburg*, The Journal of the Colonial Williamsburg Foundation, between 1986 and 1993. Though my interest in clearing up some mysteries nearer home continues, they simmer gently on back burners. It was a visit to Carter's Grove that opened my eyes to the scale of the challenges farther south. As skiers or surfers change their slopes or beaches in search of more excitement, we changed ours.

The turning point was an excellent tour of Carter's Grove in which an actor-interpreter impersonated a visit by Landon Carter. But why Landon, I wondered? Why not Carter Burwell, the builder of the mansion, or his son and successor Nathaniel Burwell, the admired plantation manager? If it had to be a Carter relative of the Burwells, why not Robert "King" Carter, who left the Grove to his grandson Carter Burwell, with the stipulation that it be named after himself? The answer was simple—Landon had written a diary about the planter's way of life.

This was the argument from analogy, which is not to be disparaged in its place. Without the analogy of Newport, where the French had billeted their troops the winter before they were quartered in Williamsburg, the Frenchman's Map would still be an unsolved mystery. Without analogies, the slave quarter at Carter's Grove could never have been reconstructed. But wherever possible, analogy should be a supplement to direct evidence, not a substitute for it.

In the faith that direct evidence might be found if we worked hard enough and roamed far enough afield, we began a series of sorties into the great Burwell dynasty, from the days when Edward Burwell, father of the Immigrant, was a keeper in Houghton Park overlooking the Vale of Bedford, and his bride Dorothy Bedell, the daughter of ancient minor gentry in Northamptonshire; through the rise of the Virginia Burwells on the Tidewater who built seven great seats; to the migration of Nathaniel Burwell and his cousins from the James River to the Shenandoah.

When we began it was not even known in Williamsburg if there was anything left of the mansion that Robert Carter Burwell, younger brother of Carter Burwell, had built across the James on Burwell's Bay. Before we finished, all sorts of evidence thought to have vanished in Virginia's wars or fires, had been recovered—letters, wills, plantation ledgers, tax records, a cryptic family tree, a whole library of Nathaniel Burwell's books, a gold Botetourt medal, a lost miniature, the undercroft of a watermill that once ground corn and wheat and distilled whiskey for Carter's Grove, an altogether clearer picture of the Burwells of Kingsmill, with their lost mansions, and a vision of the forgotten road to Yorktown on the outskirts of Williamsburg which by some miracle had not yet been lost.

Further afield, we thought we had located the English homes in which the founders of the dynasty grew up, and a classic painting of how their gilded descendants must have looked with their cricket bats in Georgian London.

We hoped that these discoveries would stimulate further finds, restore a Burwell presence in the beautiful home the Burwells had built, and intrigue the tourist with a taste for history as the art of detection.

ACKNOWLEDGMENTS

The following research institutions and their staffs are warmly thanked for their courtesy and efficiency.

In the United States, the Colonial Williamsburg Foundation, the Institute of Early American History and Culture, the Alderman Library, the Virginia Historical Society, the John Carter Brown Library, the Vassar College Library, the Yale Center for British Art, the National Portrait Gallery, the Frick Art Reference Library, and the National Park Service Center at Yorktown. In Britain, the British Library, the Public Record Office, the Bodleian Library, the Cambridge University Library, the libraries of Trinity College and Trinity Hall, Cambridge, the Lord's Cricket Ground Museum and Library, and the Courtauld Institute.

Appreciation for special services in puzzle solving is due to: Sterling Anderson, John Bedells, Linda Baumgarten, Susan Berg, Charles Lee Burwell, Lewis Burwell, Helen Byrd, Olwen, Lady Cass, Susan P. Casteras, Mary F. Goodwin, Henrietta Goodwin, Harold Gill, Graham Hood, John Ingram, Edward C. Joullian III, Pearce Grove, John Hemphill, Ellen Miles, Harry Pitt, Jacob M. Price, George Rogers, Joy Rowe, Ted Ruddock, Allen Staley, Helen Wallis, and Mark R. Wenger.

For production of this volume, credit is paid to: Vernon Wooten, cover design, Donna Sheppard, proofreading, Sondra Rose, electronic typesetting and research, and Wayne Barrett, editor.

THE LEGENDS OF CARTER'S GROVE: FACT OR FICTION?

A HISTORIC HOUSE with a romantic past is a nursery for legends. For several decades before Carter's Grove was bought by the Archibald McCreas in 1928 and clothed in its modern dress, at least three good stories had been circulating. One of these tales had its dramatic setting in the great hall and described how Colonel Banastre Tarleton, the famous English cavalryman in the Virginian campaigns of 1781, had ridden his horse up the magnificent stairs and slashed the railing with his saber. The other two told how George Washington and Thomas Jefferson had each been refused by two charming young ladies, Mary Cary and Rebecca Burwell, who subsequently married two brothers, Edward and Jaquelin Ambler. The scene of these refusals had not been specified, but Mrs. McCrea was not the lady to be deterred from inventing one. It was she who christened the southwest parlor The Refusal Room.

The earliest of these three episodes involved the youthful George Washington and Mary Cary. If there were ever a time when his roving eye fell purposefully on this young lady, it had to be in the five years between 1749 and 1754. In 1749 Mary's oldest sister, Sally Cary, settled in at Belvoir as the wife of George William Fairfax, Washington's friend and neighbor. 1754 was the year in which Mary married Edward Ambler. It would be another four years before Washington, at 27, married Martha Custis on January 6, 1759.

The four Cary sisters, Sally, Mary, Anne, and Elizabeth, were no small fry on the James River. Their grandee father, Colonel Wilson Cary, was the

Boyish countenance of Banastre Tarleton (opposite) hides the soul of a daring soldier in this 1782 mezzotint by J. R. Smith, after the painting by Sir Joshua Reynolds. Tarleton, legend says, made his mark on Carter's Grove.

naval officer for the lower river and a reputed descendant from English nobility whose brick mansion at Ceelys, overlooking Hampton Roads, was a famous center for hospitality in its day. It had its counterpart at Kingsmill, upriver from Carter's Grove where Carter Burwell's cousins were naval officers for the upper James.

Sally Cary, the oldest, has been played up as the real love in Washington's life. Mary was the second daughter; the third, Anne, married Carter Burwell's stepbrother, Robert Carter Nicholas, in 1752; the fourth, Elizabeth, became the bride in 1759 of Bryan Fairfax, the eventual heir to the Fairfax barony in England.

The belief that Washington proposed to Mary Cary is one of the curiosities of the anecdotal history of the Founding Fathers. The evidence never consisted of more than a single surviving letter in a boyish notebook of Washington's, showing that she had made quite an impression on him, and a few colorful passages about a proposal and its rejection found in a private reminiscence among the family papers of the Amblers. However, the story won all sorts of converts between the Civil War and World War I, until a debunking mood set in.

Washington's letter to an unidentified "Dear Robin" was drafted from one of the Fairfax houses in 1749 when Mary was visiting her newly married

The Refusal Room—where some believe two future Presidents were rejected— once was haunted by a ghost scattering white carnations "torn from their vases," a 1939 Associated Press article reported. Earliest portraits of the suitors: Thomas Jefferson was 43 when he sat for Mather Brown; George Washington (opposite) was 40 when Charles Willson Peale painted him.

sister, Sally. He refers to "a very agreeable young lady" who is with him, whom he identifies as "Colonel Fairfax's wife's sister," and then adds that he might "pass my time very pleasantly with her" if he were not so taken up with "the Lowland Beauty"—an unnamed love whose identity is a mystery.

He was no more than 18, Mary about 16. Though he was in no position to marry at that time, what about later? He must have seen her often in the next five years, between surveying and soldiering, either among the swarm of notabilities around the Fairfaxes at Belvoir, near Mount Vernon, or in Williamsburg. What could be more natural than a growing intimacy? She had everything he wanted in a wife—charm, character, and lots of money. But evidence there was none until 1857 when Bishop William Meade published some extracts from the Ambler family memoir in his rich storehouse of borrowed tales and personal observations called *Old Churches, Ministers and Families of Virginia.*

In his sketches of Richard Ambler, the wealthy collector of customs at Yorktown, and his sons John, Edward, and Jaquelin, Meade quoted verbatim from what he called "the family document." However, there are at least two documents, not one. The first set had belonged to Mrs. Elizabeth Carrington, no less than the daughter of Rebecca Burwell Ambler, wife of Jaquelin Ambler, whom we shall shortly meet as Jefferson's "Belinda." These papers are well known today for their charming impressions of pre-war Yorktown, their eulogies of Mrs. Carrington's parents, and their whispered scandals about the gallantries of French officers—matters which the bishop did not quote.

It is the second set, now lost, that provides the bishop with the material for his sketches of Mary Cary and her husband Edward Ambler. Obviously from internal evidence the work of Mary Cary's grandson, its author was later identified by a family historian as John Jaquelin Ambler.

The description of Washington's relationship to Mary Cary is picturesque, to say the least. It begins with the young Washington's visit to the Fairfax house where he is smitten by Mary and proceeds to pay his addresses. In time he offers his hand, but his affection is not returned and he is rejected. Where this refusal occurred is not stated. However, we are told that he had first asked Mary's father for permission to make his suit, only to be royally snubbed, with the inference that this refusal occurred at Ceelys. The old colonel had told him, "If that is your business here, sir, I wish you to leave the house, for my daughter has been accustomed to ride in her own coach."

The author could not restrain himself from adding another anecdote about George and Mary that had obviously gone the rounds. When Washington made his victory march through Williamsburg after the battle of Yorktown, he is said to have recognized Mary in the crowd and to have saluted her with a wave of his sword, only to see her faint. However, said her grandson, this story "wants confirmation," because there was nothing in his grandmother's life to suggest that she had ever regretted her marriage with Edward Ambler. He might have added a better reason, that his grandmother was dead and buried before the battle of Yorktown was begun.

WASHINGTON AND LEE UNIVERSITY

Before turning to the last years of the old lady, in which she gave a heroic account of herself as a wartime evacuee at the Ambler house, The Cottage, in Hanover County, her grandson had a final afterthought about the abortive suit. "It may be added, as a curious fact, that the lady General Washington afterward married resembled Miss Cary as much as one twin-sister ever did another."

These remarkable revelations contained inconsistencies to be sure, but they had all the appearances of a record compiled in good faith sometime before 1820 by a grandson relying on recollections from his father. Bishop Meade, of much the same generation, who knew both the Amblers and Burwells well, found nothing phony in the story. The high point in its acceptance was probably the last decade of the 19th century. A scholarly review of C. P. Keith's *Ancestry of Benjamin Harrison* (1898) contained the typical remark: "It is rather curious that the two brothers, Jaquelin and Edward Ambler (who married Mary Cary) were the successful rivals of Jefferson and Washington." A visitor to Williamsburg at that time would have the Cary townhouse pointed out to him, from which Mary Ambler was supposed to have watched the parade, and might even have been taken to the drawing room of Dr. J. D. Moncure (superintendent of the Eastern State Lunatic Asylum) where her portrait then hung.

Just how this belief was eventually eaten away by gnawing doubts is not clear. A withering blast in 1903 by well regarded Baltimore genealogist Wilson Miles Cary must have played its part. He wrote to a historian of the Carys, Louise du Bellet, hoping she would give no further circulation to the "absurd story" about Mary Cary and George Washington as "there is positively nothing in it." His grounds, as stated, seem less than conclusive to us; but her extracts in her own work from the John Jaquelin Ambler memoir that Bishop Meade had quoted—and whose authorship she had identified—deliberately omitted any reference to the condemned story.

Purveyors of entertainment who authored books about Virginia's historic houses went on repeating the old tale without bothering to say where they got it; but the scholars grew cautious. Douglas Southall Freeman conceded that Washington might have got interested in Mary Cary if he had not been in such a tangle with other young ladies, but he never mentioned the alleged proposal. James Flexner managed to write his biography of Washington's early years without even mentioning Mary Cary. If the original source, the grandson's memoir, survives today, its whereabouts are unknown to us.

It is time to remind ourselves that the grandson, as quoted by the bishop, lent no support whatever to the notion that the alleged refusal occurred at Carter's Grove. Carter's Grove was on the same plantation circuit as Ceelys, and Washington may have visited both. He certainly visited Kingsmill, a splendid center of hospitality and horsemanship under Colonel Lewis Burwell IV, and was grateful to Carter Burwell of Carter's Grove, the powerful chairman of the Military Affairs Committee, for his interest in his own career. But it is hard to imagine how the affairs of the heart might have taken Washington and Mary Cary to Carter's Grove at a time when the oldest daughter there was barely in her teens, and even harder to believe that they could have been there in the alleged circumstances without some report of such a sensational story having reached the ears of Bishop Meade through his Burwell connections. He was born in the neighborhood of Carter Hall, educated in its plantation schoolhouse, and well acquainted with several of the Burwells of Millwood who remembered their old home at Carter's Grove. If there was ever anything between the young Washington and Mary Cary, such as an unsuccessful suit, which now seems most unlikely, the refusal could only have occurred either at Ceelys or in Williamsburg.

C OMPARED with this episode, the affair between the young Thomas Jefferson and Rebecca Burwell, his fair "Belinda," offered an altogether better foothold for the propagation of a legend. Just as there is not a tittle of evidence that George and Mary were ever in each other's company at Carter's Grove, so there is none that Tom and Rebecca were. Yet the more we probe the more likely it is that the round of parties for young people might have taken them there, unless the house was temporarily closed.

The romance began in 1762, Jefferson's second and last year at the College of William and Mary, when he and his classmates were flirting with "the belles of Williamsburg" and toying with the idea of marriage. It was usual for a young planter with an adequate inheritance to marry as soon as he came of age, and it was no novelty for girls of 15 or 16 to entertain a suitor. Jefferson was 18, and no more in a position to marry than Washington had been at that age. Yet he caught the infection. Rebecca Burwell was 16. Half in earnest, half in jest, and wholly captivated by his own flights of fancy, whether he was concealing the identity of his beloved in code names or expiating on his feelings, Jefferson shared his adolescent hopes and disappointments with two of his classmates. Seven letters were written to his good friend John Page of Rosewell, the future governor; two to William Fleming. The first of these was at Christmas 1762. It described how his day had been ruined by the discovery that a leak in the roof had destroyed a silhouette of Rebecca that he kept in his watchcase. The last was written in March 1764, by which time the affair was over.

Rebecca Burwell, Carter Burwell's niece, was a great catch. Her father was Carter's older brother Lewis Burwell, of Gloucester County, who had reached the top of the political tree at the mid-century, only to be disabled by a mysterious illness. It was he who, as President of the Council, had commissioned Peter Jefferson, Thomas's father, and Joshua Fry to do their famous map of Virginia. He had died in May 1756, and, as his wife had died giving birth to Rebecca in 1746, the siblings of these Fairfield Burwells, like those of the Carter's Grove Burwells, were all raised by their Uncle William Nelson at Yorktown. Rebecca and her brother Lewis must have been living under his roof for several years before Thomas Jefferson met either of them. Just when they were followed by Carter Burwell's children we do not know—Carter died at the same time as Lewis—but it would only have been after the death of his widow, the date of which has never been determined. If this occurred in the early 1760s, which is more likely than not, then we have to remember that there might have been no functioning household at Carter's Grove in which Thomas Jefferson could have been "refused."

Jefferson must have been introduced to Rebecca by her brother Lewis Burwell, Jr., who was his classmate at the college. It also becomes clear that when he asked John Page to remember him affectionately to "the Miss Burwells" there were no less than three Miss Burwells in his circle all palpitating for a suitable suitor. Besides Rebecca, there were Frances Burwell, daughter of Robert Carter Burwell, younger brother of Carter, who had just built his seat on Burwell's Bay across the James from Carter's Grove, and Carter Burwell's own daughter Judith, now about 19. Frances Burwell would

COLONIAL WILLIAMSBURG

Banastre Tarleton "rode up the broad, low stairs on his horse, hacking at the banister rail with his sword," reads a 1915 version of the Carter's Grove legend. Mrs. Archibald McCrea, in this 1931 photograph, fingers the rail where an alleged fragment of the blade is embedded. Opposite: Tarleton's ghost, dismounted, as portrayed by Jeremy Fried.

DAVE DOODY

marry John Page before this correspondence closed, and Judith Burwell would find a husband very soon after in Samuel Griffin of Yorktown.

If marriageable daughters of Carter Burwell were living at Carter's Grove between 1762 and 1764, then the round of parties might have taken Jefferson and Rebecca there. But the end of their love affair calls for a scenario in which a refusal room at Carter's Grove has no place.

Jefferson refers to two meetings with Rebecca. The first was in the Apollo Room at the Raleigh Tavern—as famous for its balls as for its smoke-filled rooms—on October 7, 1763, when he was too tongue-tied to make his carefully rehearsed pitch. Rebecca might have spent that night at the Nelson house in Williamsburg. The second was at some unnamed place in the vicinity, and he wrongly believed it had gone well. John Page had apparently urged him to make a formal approach to her guardian, but Jefferson had thought this would be premature. He had told her that he was obliged to go to England, and how he hoped she would wait for his return when everything might move forward with her approval.

These shenanigans lost the lady. All sorts of great men have had a failure of nerve in some early crisis of their careers, whether in the lists of love or war. Perhaps this was Jefferson's problem. Certainly if he had wanted her, he should have seized his chances. Whatever his state of mind, he seems to have made no effort to see her after October 1763, and when the news of her coming marriage with Jaquelin Ambler reached him the following spring, it was not from her he heard it. There never was a face-to-face refusal. She simply walked away and married the boy next door. Jaquelin Ambler, like his brothers before him, had been raised by their father, Richard Ambler, one short block on Main Street in Yorktown from the house known to history as the "President's House" where Rebecca was raised by William Nelson.

THE SCENE for the third legend opened about 17 years later, in 1781, when the armies of Washington and Cornwallis were assembling for the Yorktown campaign.

The folklore of medieval castles was filled with stories of dashing knights spurring their steeds up flights of stairs in pursuit of enemies, or maidens, or just for the hell of it. No one should be surprised that such an exploit was fathered on the legendary Colonel Tarleton, and we would not expect that his motives, or the length of his stay at Carter's Grove, or the reactions of his involuntary hosts, would be made very clear. Some said he was trying to roust his own troopers out of the house to meet an emergency summons. However, the point of the tale is simply what he did, not why nor how he did it, except in one important particular. Such was the force of his slashing saber that a bit of it broke off and is stuck in the banister to this day!

There were procedures through which landlords in the war zone who had suffered through enemy action could claim compensation. Nathaniel Burwell, the owner of Carter's Grove, did so for farm produce that his own side had requisitioned. But there is nothing in these records to suggest an enemy occupation of Carter's Grove, or damage to its valuable furnishings, or confiscation of its cattle and crops, though foraging, not equestrian acrobatics, was the usual object of Tarleton's missions.

The whole story might be dismissed as fabrication were it not for evidence that one or more of his troopers must have prowled through the grounds. Excavations in the early 1970s under Ivor Noël Hume's supervision uncovered a brass insignia bearing Tarleton's personal crest that must have been attached to a uniform or a piece of equipment.

There were two or three periods in 1781 when English raiders might have loitered or passed by; the first in April when they were at Burwell's Ferry and Nathaniel himself was called out with his militia; the second in late June when Tarleton was there, and sheep and cattle were driven away from Kingsmill; the third and most likely period in August and September, when Tarleton's legion at Yorktown, as we are told in his journal, were foraging as far as the outskirts of Williamsburg. By this time the house, which was outside the city's defenses, was undoubtedly evacuated. No clashes are reported from there, as they were from the outpost at Burwell's Mill on the northern road to Yorktown, but that is not to say that no entry was made.

So where does this leave us? We are far from convinced that Washington made any overture to Mary Cary and certain that there was no "refusal" at Carter's Grove. We know that Jefferson was infatuated with Rebecca Burwell and might have seen her at Carter's Grove; but there is no evidence that he did nor that a "refusal" there could have occurred, given the nature of the affair. There is every probability that Tarleton's men took a look at Carter's Grove but no proof that their leader stormed up the great stairs or was even with them.

We have no reason for thinking that the Burwell family of Carter's Grove—or of Carter Hall—had ever heard of the legends. Sons and grandsons of the old colonel, who died in 1814, eventually inherited books, furnishings, and plate that had come from the Tidewater, but not these anecdotes as far as we know. The last Burwell at Carter's Grove sold the rundown mansion to the Wynnes in 1838, who held it until 1879 after many unsuccessful efforts to re-sell; but again there is no evidence that they made anything of the legends.

COLONIAL WILLIAMSBURG

Impresario Edwin G. Booth, Sr.

THE TURNING POINT seems to have come when the romanticization of the Old South after the Civil War, and all the ballyhoo that accompanied the centennials of 1776 and 1781, created a perfect climate for hatching myths. From this time on the buyers of Carter's Grove were not would-be farmers who would try to make a living out of a combined wharf-business and truck farm; they were southerners who had made money in the North and wanted an elegant home with historic associations. No sales promotion after 1879 failed to mention one or more of the legends.

A key figure in this metamorphosis was Edwin G. Booth, Sr., an ex-Virginian who had done well in Philadelphia as a lawyer and politician. Patriotic, flamboyant, every inch a promoter, he was in his element when he organized at his own expense a Virginia Pavilion at the Philadelphia Centennial Exposition of 1876. Three years later he bought Carter's Grove from the Wynnes, saying it would make a superb center for historic anniversaries. At a time when the *Century, Scribner's, Harper's* and other national magazines were filled with romantic tales about the South, Mr. Booth threw himself into plans for the Yorktown Centennial of 1881.

One exuberant celebration of his that sent a shock wave through artistic circles was his repainting of the great hall at Carter's Grove in red, white, and blue, with touches of green. Another was his sponsorship of a historical map of the lower peninsula, by the lithographic firm of Smith and Stroup in Philadelphia, with insets of the Yorktown battlefield, war heroes, and historic mansions. Of course it included a drawing of Carter's Grove, with gentle folk conversing on its terraced gardens, in the style developed by such publishers for clients with country seats.

COLONIAL WILLIAMSBURG

What, if anything, Booth got from the Wynnes is unknown. They may have been vehicles for some local, farmers' tradition about Tarleton's exploits in the neighborhood, but this is only guesswork. In a letter of 1879 to a Dr. Robert Carter Randolph of Millwood, grandson of the old Colonel Nathaniel Burwell, whom he had consulted about family history, Booth referred to the saber cut which Tarleton had made in the banister "as is supposed;" but only because he hoped that Dr. Randolph might have a chance to examine his own handsome improvements in the great hall.

He must also have been the source from which his son and daughter-in-law, Dr. and Mrs. Edwin Booth, Jr., derived their belief in the Jefferson-"Belinda" story. A letter from Mrs. Booth at Carter's Grove in 1905 to her daughter, Mrs. Henry Wise, in New York, deplored the fact that a book about the mansions on the James River, just published by her daughter's own father-in-law, should have left out the Grove, "where so much of Jefferson's time was spent with his sweetheart." She added, pathetically, because they would have to sell Carter's Grove before long, "it would have been an advertisement for this place."

So here we leave our mystery, recognizing Edwin G. Booth, Sr., as the great transmitter of the legends but without fully understanding what he added to them except *panache*. But we can be sure of one thing. He would have loved what Molly McCrea made of them.

Carter's Grove as it appeared in 1881 was owned by Edwin G. Booth, Sr. He commissioned the sketch to commemorate the Centennial of 1781.

EMBLEMS OF GENTILITY: FAMILY TREES AND A PLANTER'S COAT OF ARMS

PEDIGREES and coats of arms were no trifles in the planning of a suitably dignified way of life for a colonial aristocracy in Virginia. Even Thomas Jefferson, within a few years of composing his famous declaration of human equality, was willing to please his mother by shopping around in London for a family coat of arms. In a letter from Monticello dated February 20, 1771, he asked Thomas Adams, a merchant in London, "to search the Herald's office for the arms of my family. I have what I have been told were the family arms, but on what authority I know not. It is possible there may be none. If so I would with your assistance become a purchaser, having Sterne's word for it that a coat of arms may be purchased as cheap as any other coat."

Whether Laurence Sterne, celebrated author of *Tristram Shandy,* was responsible for this witticism or not matters less than its credibility. It suggests that the sale of honors under King George III, in the last decade of these colonies, may have been as commonplace as it was when they were founded under King James I.

Several historians have been interested in the genteel origins of the earliest emigrants. They have compiled lists of settlers in Virginia from gentry families in England, including a handful connected by blood with the nobility and the monarchy. Some of these emigrants must have brought evidence with them, such as a pedigree, painted coat of arms, signet ring, or piece of engraved plate. Yet even William Byrd II, who surely knew he was descended from King Edward III through his mother, Mary Horsemanden, felt it necessary, or entertaining, to visit the College of Heralds in 1702, be-

This article appeared in the Winter 1990-91 issue of Colonial Williamsburg *journal.*

"HERALD'S COLLEGE, THE HALL," LONDON 1808

fore his father's death would oblige him to settle in Virginia.

Vague memories of these emblems were not enough, given all the uses of heraldry in a stately home on one of the Virginia rivers. A classic description of these needs was provided by another celebrated scribbler, Daniel Defoe, when he published *The Complete English Tradesman* in 1726, about the wealthier merchants who expected the Heralds to gentrify them: "coming every day to the Herald's office, to search for the Coats of Arms of their ancestors, in order to paint them upon their coaches, and engrave them upon their furniture, or carve them upon the pediments of their new houses." He might have added, "or paste them inside their books and chisel them on their tombstones."

Heraldry was invented in the 12th century as a pictorial *Who's Who* for a feudal nobility involved in tournaments and crusades. Through the use of symbols painted on shields and helmets, it evolved as a hereditary system of personal recognition with its own intricate rules and jargon. Such medieval arts were well called "mysteries." A technical description of a coat of arms, with its subdivisions, stylized birds and animals, and exclusive use of Old French, was meant to be impenetrable to the uninitiated.

Heralds were officers in the royal household long before they were organized in a college. A chief herald, like the Garter King of Arms, was created in 1415 to preside over the display of arms on the stalls of the Knights of the Garter in the royal chapel at Windsor. Pursuivants, like Robert Dale, who features in our story, were junior heralds.

A College of Arms, or Herald's College, was chartered in 1484 by incorporating the individual heralds. The age of exploration and colonization, coinciding with the rise of gentry under Tudor and Stuart sovereigns, expanded the college. A second charter, in 1555, endowed the college with an old mansion by the Thames that burned in the Great Fire of 1666. But by 1700 a fine brick building, with the dome of the new St. Paul's towering above, had risen on what is now called Queen Victoria Street.

From 1530 to 1683, periodic visits of the heralds were made (roughly once every generation) to all the English counties, to review the applications for coats of arms and to register grants in the records of the college. There was also an ancient, eccentric court of law, the High Court of Chivalry, presided over by the Earl Marshall, to settle disputes about arms and pedigrees. It usually met, when it met at all, in the central hall of the college, which looks much the same today as it did when William Byrd II saw it.

The records of the *visitations* of each county were not to be published until the 19th and 20th centuries, but many grants of arms were abstracted for the benefit of applicants or incorporated in the manuscript collections compiled by antiquarians. An 18th-century "armory" of this kind, including the arms of Burwells and Bedells, can be seen in the Virginia Historical Society. Joan Corder's *Dictionary of Suffolk Arms*, published in 1965, provided a succinct summary of every coat of arms found in that county.

Sources such as these can tell us something about the machinery and forms of gentrification. But what do we know about the tests to be met, the rules of evidence, the scope for willful deception or innocent self-deception, the scale of influence peddling, and the enforcement of standards by either law or public opinion?

In Elizabethan England a gentleman could be defined either strictly or loosely. A rigorous antiquarian might hold that a gentleman was someone who had the right to bear arms, as attested by either a grant of the college in a previous visitation or by the evidence of long usage, ideally a century, in his family. A realist like Sir Thomas Smith, the scholar statesman, might say that a gentleman was one who could "bear the port, the charge, and countenance of a gentleman." Or as we would say, "who looked like a gentleman and could pay his way." Historians are apt to praise Smith for his wise tautology.

Historical enquiry and the scholarly interpretation of historical documents were in their infancy. Only the rare antiquarian knew how to weigh evidence that was not contemporary. The law offered some protection against willful deception in the sense that forgery was a crime and dealers could be prosecuted for the sale of spurious pedigrees. Self-deception, on the other hand, must have thrived on the gullibility of otherwise educated people. The ease with which hardheaded businessmen could persuade themselves of their descent from titled ancestors astonishes us today.

If this was the case in the mother country, we may be sure that standards were laxer on the frontier where memories were hazier, life rougher and shorter, and deeds more eloquent than words. Virginia had got along without the unwanted visitations of heralds and had no reason to fear their intrusion when their jurisdiction was decaying in England. Who was going to deny a William Fitzhugh or a Wilson Cary or a Joseph Ball the coat of arms he fancied?

A museum director in modern Virginia, familiar with the deceptions of art dealers in the sale of ancestral portraits and antiques, is frankly skeptical about the heraldry that began to bloom all over the newly built "house of taste," its coach house, and its graveyard, after 1700. "Don't we suppose," he smilingly asks, "that most of them just *assumed* their coats of arms?" Yet, in truth, nobody knows how many heads of colonial families in the formative years of the new elites approached the heralds on visits to London; or through their relatives and agents; or what information they sought; or how free they felt to use it.

It was a chance to explore some of these ambiguities through the study of a little-known family tree, itself a product of the college, that inspired this article and, at the same time, helped to solve the case of "The Lost Miniature" (see page 26). Three descendants of branches shown in the pedigree of the Burwells of Virginia were deeply involved in this adventure, though several others helped. George Harrison Burwell III, of Mount Airy, adjoining Carter Hall in Millwood, Clarke County, deserves the credit for the only mention in print this intriguing artifact has ever had. It was hanging in his home in 1961 when he finished writing a sketch of his ancestor, Carter Burwell, the builder of Carter's Grove. This was when Colonial Williamsburg was planning to take over the plantation and its beautiful mansion.

The sketch was intended for family and friends; G. H. Burwell III did not bother to explain how he came by the heirloom, which he refers to as "the old Alverd-Burwell Tree of obscure origin." Yet he was not unmindful of the interest that Colonial Williamsburg might take in this possession, so he quoted in full the long legend at the foot, "A Genealogical Arbor of the ancient Family of Burwell of Sutton in the County of Suffolk," which Robert Dale, whose full name and title—"Blanch Lion Pursuivant"—he could not quite make out, had put together in 1698. He undoubtedly hoped that experts at Williamsburg might tell him what it had to do with his own family, and offer to buy it.

I never met this Burwell, who died in 1970, but I could easily understand his predicament. Who were these Suffolk Burwells? All the Burwells of Virginia knew that their ancestors came from Bedfordshire and Northamptonshire. The tomb of Lewis Burwell the Immigrant said so. Historian T. J. Wertenbaker had confirmed the family tradition. How could the strangers, in all these little circles on the tree, be ancestors of his? He would go to his grave, in spite of repeated appeals to the experts, as much in the dark as he had always been.

About a decade later, as I was leaving for a tour through the "Burwell

Country" to the north and northeast of London in search of their English roots, I got to know Lewis Burwell of Floyd, Virginia, who was burning to see the old Alverd-Burwell Tree, which he and his cousin, Virginia Krog, of the Kingsmill Burwells, had also read about in the sketch of Carter Burwell.

Unlike their Millwood cousin, they were self-taught students of family genealogy and heraldry who were determined to clear the record of all its accumulated rubbish. They had satisfied themselves through personal inspection of the early tombs, careful reading of the published *Visitations of Suffolk*, and correspondence with county record offices in England, that the Virginia Burwells, male and female, had never used any arms except the Suffolk arms, no matter what several high priests of heraldry in America might have published to the contrary. Consultants approved by the College of Heralds had told them very little they had not found out for themselves, and seemed never to have heard of Robert Dale's Alverd-Burwell Tree, which by this time had disappeared from Mount Airy. Would it offer any support for their favorite theory of a blood relationship between the Bedfordshire and the Suffolk Burwells, posited on the ingenious suggestion that Edward, or Edmund, Burwell of Harlington in Bedfordshire, grandfather of Lewis Burwell the Immigrant, might easily have been one of those younger sons of Edmund Burwell of Sutton and his wife, Margery Alverd, whom the Heralds had been obliged to leave nameless?

The neatness of this proposal is at once apparent when we locate the two circles on the third branch, to the left of the eldest son, William Burwell of Sutton, which are simply inscribed "Burwell a younger son." But a first step in seeking the necessary proof would be to locate the missing tree.

It was in the Millwood home, The Vineyard, of the third descendant, Charles Lee Burwell, that the search for both elusive heirlooms really ended. Charles had been born at Carter Hall during the ownership of his father Townsend Burwell, half-brother of G. H. Burwell III. He had inherited from his uncle on his death in 1970 some valuable memorabilia, such as plantation ledgers from both Carter's Grove and Carter Hall, and the gold Botetourt medal won by Colonel Nathaniel Burwell as a student at the College of William and Mary. These were given either to the Colonial Williamsburg Foundation or to the local museum at Berryville, and I was invited to The Vineyard to see if Uncle George's papers had anything of interest.

Letters to Uncle George from his Randolph cousins showed that the peripatetic "Genealogical Arbor" and the "Lost Miniature" of Colonel Burwell had been owned by the Randolphs for a century and a half before they were loaned—or perhaps given—to the Clarke County cousins at Mount Airy. There was even a photograph of the tree that Uncle George had given to his nephew in anticipation of its eventual return to the Randolphs.

It was a matter of moments to confirm by telephone that George Harrison's widow had returned the tree to Robert Carter Randolph, fifth of that name, in Seattle, Washington, while the miniature had been sent for safekeeping to his mother, Mrs. A. R. Meredith, at Woodlands Plantation, Brodnax, Virginia. Subsequently I had the pleasure of meeting Mrs. Meredith and iden-

Carved in stone, the arms of
Walpole and Burwell adorn
the pediment of the old stables
at Houghton (right), the prime
minister's birthplace.
Engraved on the tomb of
Nathaniel Burwell in
Abingdon churchyard (below)
is the burr-leaf crest that
replaced the earlier griffin.
Less enduring, the watercolor
(opposite) is a fake coat of the
Burwells. The crest was used
briefly in the 18th century.

COURTESY LEWIS BURWELL

tifying the miniature.

Seeing the family tree at Colonial Williamsburg—where photographic reproductions will be made, while it is on loan, to hang at Carter's Grove—left vivid first impressions. How rosy cheeked it still looked after three centuries—almost as fresh as when Robert Dale's heraldic artist first painted it. It is older than all the public buildings in Williamsburg, except Bruton Parish Church, and probably older than the imported tombstones that replaced the markers in the family graveyard at Fairfield. Among Burwell memorabilia only a few wills and deeds in the record offices of Virginia or southern England are older.

How extraordinary that so little is known about the tree's origins and significance. Who ordered it? What use was made of it? What did later generations think about it? Did it hang honorably in the halls of all those Burwell homes? Or gather dust in the attics? For all the notice it seems to have received, inside or outside the family, it might never have existed.

Or were there reasons for not wanting to advertise its existence? How could it have been ignored when Burwell genealogies were being compiled at the end of the last century? Or when contradictory views of the "real" Burwell arms were still spreading confusion into the 1960s? Or when the research staff at Williamsburg was collecting charts and illustrations for its documentary history of Carter's Grove? Or were we being fooled by appearances? We decided to pursue these questions with whatever combination of words, charts, and pictures seemed best, and to make our own "search of the Herald's Office" before reporting our findings.

First, who ordered the tree? The obvious candidate is Major Lewis Burwell II (ca 1651-1710), a co-founder of one of the great colonial dynasties. Each of his three sons who reached adulthood would have his own seat: Nathaniel at Fairfield, where a newly finished mansion had replaced the pioneer homestead; James, at King's Creek, in the mansion inherited from Nathaniel Bacon, president of the Council, whose niece, Abigail Smith, was the major's first wife; and Lewis at Kingsmill, on more of the Bacon acreage as soon as he was old enough to build for himself. Six daughters of the major had married into the top families, and there were probably expectations before the major died of more seats for boys from Robert "King" Carter's bounty.

The major had all those insistent heraldic needs already described. He must have asked the heralds if they had any record of a grant of arms to the Burwells, and what he received was not only this splendid, painted pedigree of the Suffolk Burwells with its three coats of arms, but also—one of several surprises at Woodlands—a separate, signed certificate from Robert Dale, so worn and torn it was only half legible. If George Harrison Burwell had seen this, it had made no impression; but a Randolph widow had lovingly pasted the fragments together when she was sorting her husbands's papers in the 1930s and scribbled, "Very old and interesting!"

Second, how did the major use this information? If anything seems certain, in this game of deductions from circumstantial evidence, it is that he, and his immediate descendants, and their remote descendants if they kept their Burwell wits about them, found in the coats of arms exactly what they were looking for. Fresh from the fountain of honor in every sparkling detail in 1698, and still fresh in the 1990s, here was a perfect model for the family arms. If the three coats that dominate the composition are compared, the same basic coat will be seen in all of them; most simply, on the trunk, below the name of Thomas Alverd; then, with all the trimmings of mantle, helmet, and crest, at the left of the trunk; and finally, in two of the four quarters of the matching shield on the right, though with a different crest.

In plain English, the coat consists of a silver (argent) shield divided by a blue (azure) St. Andrew's cross (saltire) into four sections, with a red (gules) griffin's head, as if torn off from its body (erased) in each corner, a gold (or) leopard's face at the center of the cross, and a gold lozenge in the center of each arm. The crest was the same griffin's head.

These are the arms of Thomas Alverd, merchant of Ipswich, and protégé of his city's greatest son, Cardinal Thomas Wolsey, under whose wing he was made groom of the bedchamber and ambassador to France. He died in 1534, four years after Wolsey's arrest for treason and death en route to London to face his accusers.

The names of his five daughters and co-heirs fill the bottom branch of the tree, with the marriage of Margery Alverd to Edmund Burwell at the center. All the sisters married into the rising gentry.

Robert Dale did not instruct his staff painter to label the two big coats. It was the first Randolph owner who scribbled a number and a name under each when he autographed his find in 1835. But Dale's signed certificate attested that the big coat on the left had been granted to William Burwell of Sutton in 1587 by Sir William Dethick, a Garter King of Arms in Elizabeth's reign, and that the arms involved were those of Thomas Alverd, whose daughter was William Burwell's mother.

The reader will see that the names inscribed in the little circles are often accompanied by dates, and may guess correctly that these are citations of visitations. In the case of William Burwell of Sutton, only "living in 1587" is inscribed, but the major knew from Dale's certificate that this was the date of Dethick's grant.

The same sort of clue accompanies the name of Sir Geoffrey Burwell of Rougham Place, higher up the tree on the right—"living at the time of the Visitation of 1664." The reader can consult the published edition of this visitation for the record of a grant to Sir Geoffrey and find a reproduction of the big coat on the right of our tree. It is in black and white but omits details like the leopard's face and the lozenges; otherwise it is the same. The major had no such handy work of reference as we do, but he had ways of knowing through his Suffolk connections abut this second coat.

Sir Geoffrey had presumably applied to the herald's office for a distinctively Burwell coat that would preserve the Alverd arms in the secondary position, but find a fitting symbol for the rising Burwells in the primary position. Heraldry encouraged its own sense of humor. What better than a punning use of the leaves of the burr-oak, in the first and third quarters of the shield, separated by a chevron of ermine, and in the new crest, where a lion's paw grasps three burr leaves?

The major and his three sons, judged by all that survives of their heraldry, followed the model of the earlier Burwell coat, with its unquartered Alverd arms, as granted by Dethick—the only recognized Burwell coat in their region when their family emigrated. The evidence all comes from engraved tombs—in the churchyard at Abingdon, where the Fairfield tombs were reconstructed in 1911; on the original tomb of James Burwell at King's Creek, as directed by his will of 1718 and now preserved by the U. S. Navy in its Cheatham Annex; and on the tomb of Elizabeth Burwell Harrison in Westover Church.

More evidence, either documentary or archaeological, may still surface. The communion silver given by the major to Abingdon Church and defaced in the Rosewell fire of 1916, may have borne his crest, a griffin's head, as reported to G. H. Burwell by a lady who used to clean it. The coat of arms that hung at King's Creek when James died must have been this coat, but no description survives.

However, there is more than enough evidence to uphold the testimony of our consultant, Lewis Burwell of Floyd. The only recorded deviation from the model was the adoption of a new crest on the tombs of both James Burwell (d. 1718) and Nathaniel Burwell (d. 1721); in each case a twig of three burr leaves clasped in a lion's paw replaced the griffin's head, to which later generations would return. The two brothers had both visited England in the first decade of the new century and may well have seen the arms granted to Sir Geoffrey of Rougham in 1664, which carried this crest, and are preserved to this day on a monument in Rougham Church.

Had the Virginia Burwells any right to wear these Suffolk arms, or did they just "assume" them? A strict constructionist would say they had no right to do so, unless registration by the heralds or long usage by a Bedfordshire branch before it left England could be demonstrated. A blood relationship as

BURWELL COUNTRY

WALES

ENGLAND

Northampton

Bedford

Hunts

Cambridge

Norfolk

Suffolk

Hertford

Essex

LONDON

English Channel

LOUIS LUEDTKE

OVERLEAF: Family trees trace lineages of the Suffolk and Virginia Burwells. At left is Robert Dale's Alverd-Burwell Tree, 1698, as autographed by Dr. Robert Carter Randolph in 1835 (reproduced courtesy of the Randolph family). Opposite, the Burwells of Virginia Tree was compiled by Lewis Burwell of Floyd, Virginia, and drawn by Louis Luedtke.

*T*HE BURWELLS *and their allied families came from a group of eight counties to the north and northeast of London; the eastern half composing East Anglia, those inland usually called "home counties." The university town of Cambridge was the rough center of this region. There is an Anglo-Saxon village called Burwell near the borders of Cambridgeshire and Suffolk.*

Two generations of Burwells, with their Wingate connections had lived, before Dorothy Bedell Burwell and her second husband Roger Wingate emigrated, in a cluster of Bedfordshire villages near Ampthill and Houghton Park. Villages like Catsworth and Hammerton on the borders of Huntingdon and Northamptonshire had long been home for the Bedells. John Burwell, founder of the Connecticut Burwells, was raised across the Hertfordshire border, within a few miles of the Bedfordshire Burwells. The more affluent Suffolk Burwells, with their Alverd pedigree, came from the seats named on "The Old Family Tree." It was Mary Burwell, heiress of Sir Geoffrey Burwell, who became the mother of prime minister Sir Robert Walpole.

The illustrious house of Bacon, founded by Sir Nicholas Bacon and embellished by Francis, Lord Bacon, had impressive seats in Suffolk, Hertfordshire, and Norfolk. The Nathaniel Bacons who made names for themselves in Virginia were descended from one of Sir Nicholas Bacon's brothers, a London merchant, and raised as sons of minor gentry in Suffolk villages. Abigail Smith, heiress of Nathaniel Bacon, Sr., who married Lewis Burwell II, came from a merchant home in Colchester, Essex.

A Genealogical Arbor of the ancient Family of BURWELL of Sutton in the County of SUFFOLK: as also of Woodbridge and Rougham in the same County; of Dorchester in Com. Dorset and of the City of Durham, branch'd from that Flourishing Stock.

Faithfully Collected from the several Visitation Books of their Counties, and other Manuscripts remaining in the Heralds Office London, Dale Gent. Branch ... Dep. Register of the College of Arms, 1698.

Robert C. Randolph M.D.
New Market
Clark County
A.D. 1835.

Burwell No. 1

No. 2 Alverd

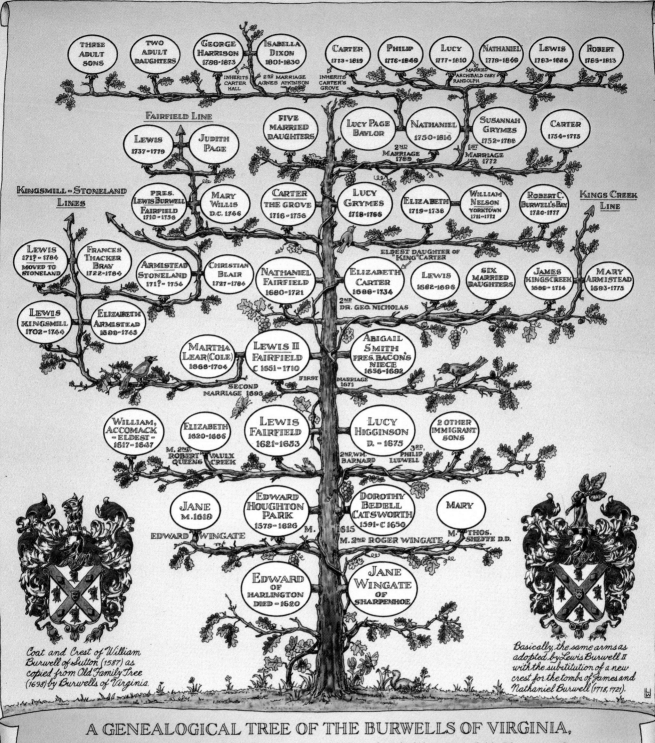

A GENEALOGICAL TREE OF THE BURWELLS OF VIRGINIA,

as descended from Bedfordshire, England, through seats in Virginia at Fairfield, Gloucester Co.,
King's Creek, York Co., Kingsmill and Carter's Grove, James City Co., Stoneland, Mecklenburg Co.,
Burwell's Bay, Isle of Wight Co., and Carter Hall, Frederick Co.

Compiled by Lewis Burwell of Floyd, Va., and drawn by Louis Luedtke 1990

Coat and Crest of William
Burwell of Sutton (1587) as
copied from Old Family Tree
(1698) by Burwells of Virginia.

Basically, the same arms as
adopted by Lewis Burwell II
with the substitution of a new
crest for the tombs of James and
Nathaniel Burwell (1718, 1721).

postulated by the Burwell-Krog team, in which the Bedfordshire grandfather of Lewis Burwell I was a younger brother of William Burwell of Sutton, Suffolk, would have met this standard. But it required one of the two unnamed brothers on Dale's tree to be called Edward or Edmund. Alas, William's will of March 3, 1595, at Ipswich, showed that one was John, the other Richard.

Still, there are two or three serious questions to be raised before the possibility of a Suffolk linkage is ruled out. First, given all the major's Suffolk connections through his first wife Abigail Smith, his duties as an executor under the will of her uncle, Nathaniel Bacon, and the probability that his own sons and grandsons would run into the Suffolk Burwells in London or Cambridge, how would the "assumption" of their arms sit with them? Second, if the Burwells of Bedfordshire cannot be traced in the gentry records of that county behind Edward Burwell of Harlington, grandfather of Lewis Burwell I, where did they come from? They are only mentioned in the *Visitations of Bedfordshire* because they married into a 200-year-old family of Wingates. Could they have mushroomed overnight from the yeomanry?

IN MY SEARCH for Burwell roots, I had run into a family of yeoman Burwells who lived near the church of Houghton Conquest and were good friends of the vicar. Edward Burwell, father of Lewis I, must have known them well. But there was nothing about their modest wills, or their illiteracy, to make them eligible husbands for female Wingates or Bedells, whose ancestors had been buried for two centuries as country squires in the chancels of their village churches.

An heirloom in Dorothy Bedell's home was one of those gold signet rings that passed from father to eldest son, leaving an imprint of the family arms that can still be seen on Northamptonshire deeds today. Her brother Gabriel, was a younger son in a huge family, sailed on the James River with Captain John Smith and looked like a regular "gallant"—a real gentleman. Her husband, Edward Burwell, progenitor of all the Virginia Burwells, may have been born in Harlington House, famous as the home of Francis Wingate in which John Bunyan was convicted for unlawful preaching, and was certainly Keeper of the Park at Houghton House, near Ampthill, the probable inspiration for Bunyan's vision of the House Beautiful at the summit of the Hill Difficulty. What if his principal duty was to see that there were enough prime deer in the park to satisfy the appetite of King James I in his visits to his employers, the Countess of Pembroke, or her successor, Lord Thomas Bruce? He was still styled Edward Burwell, gentleman, in all the deeds.

A final reason for not dismissing the possibility of a blood tie with the Suffolk Burwells are the reports circulating in the 1750s that Carter Burwell had invoked a kinship with the Walpoles to improve his chances of an appointment to the Council. Could his elder brother Lewis, himself president of the Council, have known of these ties ever since his student days at Cambridge? If so, what a conversation piece the old family tree would have made at Carter's Grove or Fairfield, with Sir Geoffrey Burwell's daughter perched on the top branch before she flew off to marry a Norfolk squire and become the mother of a prime minister.

There is a striking similarity between this intriguing conundrum in Burwell heraldry and a similar puzzle in the arms brought to Millinbeck on the Northern Neck by Joseph Ball, George Washington's maternal grandfather. He is said to have brought to these Virginia shores about 1650 a coat of arms painted on parchment, which he made the model for the family arms. At last report, it was still in the hands of descendants. Experts in heraldry have identified these arms as the registered coat of Balls in Northamptonshire, but no matter how hard they have tried, they have yet to demonstrate any connection between the Virginia Balls and the Northamptonshire Balls. Perhaps only George Washington himself, who felt even less protective about his ancestry than Jefferson, would be inclined to say, "Enough is enough. What if they were assumed?"

FROM THE DEATH of Carter Burwell in 1756 through the long life of his son Nathaniel, there is no trace of the tree until it surfaces at Newmarket, Clarke County, in 1835, in the home of Dr. Robert Carter Randolph, who, family tradition says, found it "in the garret" at Carter Hall. The occasion was probably a little family auction held by the executors long after the colonel's death, when the heirs had a chance to bid on his books and furniture. Dr. Randolph bought Carter Burwell's Bible and prayer book, but was probably allowed to keep the tree on the principle of "finders, keepers," as no sale was recorded.

He was in several ways ideally qualified to struggle with its puzzles. He had been born and raised in Carter Hall where his father, Archibald Cary Randolph, famous professor of horse flesh, had moved in. Robert gave up the Navy for a country practice in the idyllic community of Millwood, surrounded by all his transplanted tidewater cousins, where he found a second vocation as clerk of the vestry of the Old Chapel. An avid collector and scribbler, his obituaries are a treasury of family history. Born a generation earlier, he would have imbibed everything his grandfather, the old colonel, could have told him about Carter's Grove and Carter Hall, including the stories about this tree. As it was, the best thing he could do was to hand it on, a valued heirloom to successors who would make more of it. It was he who always referred to it as "The Old Family Tree."

He has been unfairly criticized by the Williamsburg staff of the 1960s for his labeling of the two big coats, which was done in 1835, without the benefit of a published *Visitation of Suffolk*, and before he had ever seen the Tidewater tombs. Even so, there was nothing wrong about "Burwell No. 1" as a tag for the first coat granted to the Burwells. His only error was to label the second coat "Alverd," which was obviously more than that, instead of "Burwell quartering Alverd."

Did this tree really contribute nothing to the modern understanding of Burwell arms, or are we misled by appearances? The short answer is that its contribution was never acknowledged, even by those who were in the best position to do so, much to the confusion of all concerned. But its hidden hand was there to undo the damage in the end.

In 1881 R. A. Brock, of the Virginia Historical Society, introduced a competing view of the Burwell arms that was to run its misguided course for the next century. The crest is the now familiar twig of burr leaves, registered by Sir Geoffrey Burwell of Rougham, but the coat is a "paly of six" vertical stripes, alternately silver and black, crossed by a gold "bend" with a blue teal's head at the center. Dr. Blair Burwell of Richmond, a Kingsmill descendant, was cited as the authority.

In 1907 Peter Mayo erected a bronze mural tablet in Bruton Parish Church to the memory of his Mayo and Burwell ancestors in the Revolution. A tiny but faithful casting of the Burwell coat granted by Dethick, complete with its leopard face and lozenges, can be clearly recognized in the bottom right-hand corner. In the next year, 1908, his brother-in-law, G. H. Burwell II, published a genealogy, *Record of the Burwell Family*, which used the same coat, saying it was an enlargement of the arms on the Bruton tablet.

Not a word was said about the old family tree in these presentations. Was it once again lost in either mystery or obscurity? Not at all. It was hanging on the walls of Powhatan, Peter Mayo's own summer residence, which had become home for the Randolphs after the Doctor's death in 1887. Mayo had obviously used it for exactly the same reason that Major Lewis Burwell II had bought it two centuries earlier, as a model for the family arms.

In 1964 Edward M. Riley, director of research in Williamsburg, approved a genealogical chart of the Burwells with the correct illustration of the Burwell arms, which we may infer was taken from the Burwell *Record*. But there was neither citation nor explanation.

The climax in this muddle of information and noninformation came in 1968 when Uncle George persuaded Riley to let his staff give the tree a thorough going-over. In due course it came back to Mount Airy with a long "transcript and evaluation" that could only have disappointed all concerned. The transcript was acceptable. The evaluation showed no awareness of any controversy, addressed none of the puzzles that have perplexed me, never mentioned William Dethick or the recent *Dictionary of Suffolk Arms*, and charged Dr. Randolph with being mixed up.

Uncle George had hoped for more. The staff could hardly have offered less. The whole subject was so quietly buried that I knew nothing about it until I stumbled on a typescript of the evaluation among the papers at The Vineyard. All this occurred while John L. Blair, author of "The Rise of the Burwells" in the *Virginia Magazine* (1964), admitted he was unable to decide between the competing coats; and while the Society was ready to exhibit a watercolor of the fake one without comment, when it arrived as a bequest from a descendant of the colonel's son, Lewis, in 1972.

Finally, did our own "search of the Herald's Office" yield anything new? There was nothing to be learned about how the request had been initiated, to whom the tree was sent, or what restrictions, if any, were suggested about its use. There was a pedigree of the Burwells of Suffolk, as prepared by Robert Dale, which was obviously the basis for the tree. It added nothing to or subtracted anything from the information we already had, from the long legend at the bottom to the smallest detail inside the circles, except by listing on the cover the references to records in the college library. All the staff painter had to do was to turn this chart, with its verbal instructions, into our genealogical arbor.

A certified copy, signed May 17, 1990, was obtained for Williamsburg records from Terence McCarthy, Bluemantle Pursuivant of Arms. No evidence was forthcoming about any linkage between the Suffolk Burwells and the Bedfordshire Burwells, but my indispensable consultant at the office, John Bedells, himself a descendant of the Bedells who concern us in this story, is as reluctant to give up this theory as Lewis Burwell of Floyd. It must be further back than was posited, he suggested, and perhaps with ties to the yeomanry as well as the gentry, and may never be found.

New to me, and most welcome, was a complete transcript of the grant made to William Burwell of Sutton in 1587 by William Dethick, Garter King of Arms. Robert Dale had quoted enough of this document in his certificate of 1698 that accompanied his tree to Virginia to make it clear that he had studied the original grant in Sir William's "very Orthography," but he had omitted several lines, and others included are now mutilated. No office copy of his certificate survives today.

More astonishing by far was the reported reaction of the present Garter King of Arms, Sir Colin Cole, when he was shown his predecessor's grant of the Alverd Arms in precisely the same form to another family, the Burwells, while Alverds were still alive to claim an exclusive right to them. He had never seen a case like it. He could only think that Dethick had blundered. If so, it would not be the last time. Though well qualified by both birth and capacity—his father was a Garter King of Arms—he was eventually fired for his arbitrariness. Perhaps he intended to confirm the Alverd arms as a quartering to new arms for William Burwell of Sutton, of the sort that Sir Geoffrey of Rougham eventually received. If so, he forgot the main business.

The mere layman can add nothing to the opinions of a Garter King of Arms on his own turf. But I was interested to see that Dethick does not specifically say in his grant that Burwell had requested, or was being given, the Alverd coat of arms. It was Robert Dale, in his certificate of 1698, who pointed out in no uncertain terms that this was what he got.

So ends our report, with what Mark Twain might have called "a twist in the tail." Embedded in this puzzling heirloom is now a double paradox. The Burwells of Virginia have still to justify their assumption of Suffolk arms, which the Burwells of Suffolk had no right to accept in the first place.

Such were the pitfalls in a planter's search for a coat of arms.

THE LOST MINIATURE OF THE OLD COLONEL

NO HEIRLOOM in a Virginia mansion is the subject of more ambiguity than the family portrait. For decades an oil painting of "the old Colonel" has hung in the hall. For decades visitors have been told to look at his long nose or his short neck. "That is a family characteristic," their host explains. "We all have it." Then the house changes hands, the portrait disappears, and the enquirer discovers that it was not the old colonel after all.

The villain in this tragi-comedy is the art dealer who manufactures ancestors on order if the price is right, after cooking up a suitable pedigree for the portrait. Burwell descendants have been the victims of this sort of chicanery on more than one occasion. Their most famous ancestor was Lucy Higginson, the progenitrix of all the Virginia Burwells through her first husband, Lewis the Immigrant, and also of all the Virginia Ludwells through her third husband, Philip Ludwell. No portrait of Lucy was known to exist before Gerard B. Lambert bought Carter Hall and embarked on its elegant restoration, but it was not long before one materialized.

Another purchase of Mr. Lambert's was a portrait of Elizabeth Carter, daughter of Robert "King" Carter and the progenitrix through her son Carter Burwell of all the Burwells of Carter's Grove and Carter Hall. This painting, attributed to the Swede, Gustavus Hesselius, one of the best known of the artists who visited colonial Virginia, enjoyed a place of honor at Carter Hall until Mr. Lambert's acquisitions were sold at a public auction by Sotheby Parke Bernet in 1976.

Both these portraits succumbed to what is best called "the identity

This article appeared in the Winter 1990-91 issue of Colonial Williamsburg *journal.*

crisis in the portrait gallery." The supposed portrait of Lucy Higginson was reclassified as a portrait of Lady Frances Berkeley, the widow of Governor William Berkeley whom Philip Ludwell married after he lost Lucy, and the supposed Elizabeth Carter, when last heard from, had sunk to the grade of "subject and artist unknown."

In each of these cases, and in two others where the alleged subjects were also distinguished members of the Burwell family, Lewis Burwell of Gloucester County and his wife Frances Willis, the fabrications were no older than the '20s and '30s of this century, and the clue to the alleged identity was money. This, however, was by no means true of the identity crisis in store for the portrait in oils of Nathaniel Burwell of Carter's Grove and Carter Hall.

Here the 20th-century owners, before it was given to the Clarke County Historical Association in 1981, were descendants of George Harrison Burwell I, who was 15 when his father, the old colonel, died in 1814. George inherited Carter Hall in 1829, shared it with the colonel's widow until she died in 1843, lived there in great style until the Civil War devastated his class, and only died in 1873. No specific reference to the portrait has come down to us from his day, but his son G. H. Burwell II, who was 25 when his father died and lived on until 1926, never doubted that it was an authentic likeness of his grandfather.

It was he who sold Carter Hall in the 1880s and moved to Mount Airy, a few hundred yards away, where his sons G. H. Burwell III and

Mann Page III of Mansfield
(below) left this miniature to
comfort his widow. Was this
an example for Colonel
Nathaniel Burwell to follow?
The oil painting (right) might
be titled "Subject Unknown,
Artist Unknown." Is it a
portrait of Colonel Burwell
from a lost miniature?

VIRGINIA
HISTORICAL SOCIETY

PHOTO BY DAVE DOODY

REDWOOD LIBRARY, NEWPORT, R. I.
Charles Bird King, self-portrait

Townsend were born. Both inherited the same tradition. Charles Lee Burwell, born in 1917 at Carter Hall, distinctly remembers Sunday dinners at Mount Airy with his grandfather, his father, and his Uncle George, and was well aware, even at that tender age, that the portrait in the hall was that of his great-great-grandfather, the old colonel. When G. H. Burwell II died in 1926, the portrait stayed at Mount Airy with G. H. Burwell III, while his half-brother Townsend had a copy made for Carter Hall.

All these witnesses had been told that the portrait had been painted by Charles Bird King, a highly regarded painter from Newport, Rhode Island, who was painting portraits in the South during the last two years of the colonel's life and continued to do so for many years. Many of his portraits can be admired at the Redwood Library, in his hometown, which was left his own collection in his will. The family had also been told that the same artist was responsible for the portrait of the colonel's son Nathaniel that has hung at Saratoga in Boyce, Clarke County, since it was painted. These attributions were reported by Everard Kidder Meade, of Millwood, well known for a catalog of portraits compiled for the Clarke County Historical Association in 1940 and sent to the Frick Art Reference Library. However, it should be clearly understood that the sitter in a family portrait is always far more important to a Virginia family than the identity of its artist.

T HERE MATTERS stood until the art historians and curators decided to look more closely into them. It was the simple attribution of the colonel's portrait to King that first aroused their skepticism. The earliest allusion to the portrait in the Frick Art Reference Library was in 1922-23, when it was attributed to King by Lawrence Park but described as "a copy from a miniature." Park's notes, together with whatever authorities he may have cited, have been lost by the library, but in 1978 the staff was still following his judgment by listing it as a copy by King "after an unknown artist."

At that time Andrew J. Cosentino, who had done a doctoral dissertation on King, published his catalog of King's paintings in which the Burwell portrait was listed among the "known Works," with the comment, "possibly a copy of a lost miniature." However, Cosentino also added, "attribution doubtful." In time he seems to have grown more skeptical about any involvement in the portrait by King, but he is said never to have seen the portrait itself, only a poor photograph.

Worse was to follow. Twice offered to the Colonial Williamsburg Foundation, it was twice declined. George Harrison Burwell III seems to have offered it for sale before his death in 1970, but the reasons for its refusal at that time are not available. The second refusal of 1979, following an offer by the heirs to make it a charitable gift to the Foundation, is well documented. The portrait was not up to museum quality; it was almost certainly not the work of King; it may have been no older than its late 19th-century frame; it had recently been badly restored; and there was no evidence that the subject was Colonel Nathaniel Burwell.

I had once coined my own epitaph for the colonel in a moment of frustration with how little seemed to have been done by posterity to preserve his memory: "Lucky in life, but lost to history." He had impressed his contemporaries, including Thomas Jefferson, as an able, decent, wise man. To rescue his portrait from the final ignominy of "artist unknown, subject unknown" was one thing I could try to do for him.

Everything hung on the chance that the so-called lost miniature might be recovered. Park's observation that the portrait was copied from a miniature seemed to be borne out by a certain stiffness in the treatment. There is a world of difference, for instance, between the vitality of King's self-portrait

SARATOGA AT MILLWOOD
Nathaniel Burwell of Saratoga

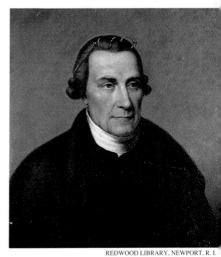

REDWOOD LIBRARY, NEWPORT, R. I.
Patrick Henry, by C. B. King, probably from the same miniature as used by Thomas Sully in 1815.

COLONIAL WILLIAMSBURG

of 1815 that hangs in the Redwood Library in Newport and the adjacent portrait of Patrick Henry, which King painted in 1825 from a miniature under the direction of the family. None of the skeptics had enquired if any of the numerous descendants of the colonel had heard of such a miniature.

One of these descendants was Louise Patten, who left to the Virginia Historical Society a miniature of Mann Page III of Mansfield, intimate friend and relative of Nathaniel. They were cousins by birth and contemporaries at college, who became brothers-in-law in 1789 when Nathaniel married his second wife, Lucy Page Baylor, at Mansfield. Mann Page III predeceased the colonel in 1803, leaving his miniature to his daughter Maria Mann, who married Lewis, the colonel's son.

With my mind on miniatures, my eye was caught by the obvious similarity between Page's attire and that of the subject of the Burwell portrait. Only Page's vest, a delicate yellow flecked with rust, was different. Could a similar miniature of the colonel's have descended through another line?

It could and had, as I have described elsewhere in tracing the old family tree from the Burwells at Mount Airy to the Randolphs at Woodlands. When I spoke to Mrs. A. R. Meredith, formerly Mrs. Robert Carter Randolph III, over the phone she felt she could not be positive about the subject of the miniature but was quite sure it had never been lost. "It was only a long time coming home," she exclaimed cheerfully.

The descent, as eventually pieced together, had been to the colonel's daughter Lucy, wife of Archibald Cary Randolph; to her son Dr. Robert Carter Randolph (1807-87), who found the tree; from him to his daughter-in-law Eliza Page Burwell, wife of Thomas Hugh Burwell Randolph (1843-1900); then to their son, another Dr. Robert Carter Randolph (1869-1928), during whose lifetime at Powhatan, the Mayo summer home, it must have come to the notice of Park.

I T SHOULD NOT perhaps surprise us that G. H. Burwell III seems never to have grasped the full significance of either heirloom, in spite of their extended stay in his home and his own ambitions as a family historian. It no more occurred to him to mention the borrowed miniature, with its striking resemblance to the portrait he knew so well, than to perceive that the "Ge-

Charles Lee Burwell (below) stands in front of Carter Hall, his birthplace, where the Burwell miniature was painted and the old family tree found. The mansion (bottom) and Carter's Grove (opposite, above) are reminders of one of America's great family dynasties.

DAVE DOODY

nealogical Arbor" of the Suffolk Burwells must have been the source of his own family's coat of arms.

We had only to see the miniature to realize that our search was over. If the colonel looks less than well, it is because he is an ailing old man of 63, already wasting from the disease that will wear him out in two more years.

Enclosed in the familiar oval copper case, with a glass front, the colonel's miniature was slightly larger than Mann Page's, being 7.3 cm by 5.8 cm. In the rear, where a monogram was often engraved on the copper back, an oval window revealed an S-shaped lock of hair against a mother-of-pearl background, secured with one little pearl at the center and a second one lower down. The attire was the familiar male attire in the age of Washington and Jefferson, the tight, white muslin stock around the throat to keep a republican's head as high as his hopes, a frilled white shirt peeping or billowing out below, a buttoned vest or waistcoat with turned-down lapels, and a massive frock coat with its own row of big buttons down the front and its deep collar rising at the back of the neck almost to the level of the ears. Farther down there would be knee breeches, silk stockings, and buckled shoes, but of course the bust was cut off long before that. St. Mémin, who did a roaring business at Richmond in the first decade of the new century, struck off dozens of profiles in this costume, one of them, in 1805, of the colonel's own son, Carter.

Comparing the miniature with the portrait, the head, stock, shirt, vest, and frock coat down to and including the fourth big button shows them to be virtually identical. Nose and mouth are slightly different in the miniature, and the body is turned more to the front. The painter of the portrait has seated Nathaniel sideways on an upholstered chair and added his arms, the right arm resting on the arm of the chair with book in hand, the left hand tucked inside the frock coat. Inscribed on the rear of the case is "J Warrell 1812."

JAMES WARRELL was an artist-entrepreneur who left his mark on art history in Virginia. He was brought here from England as a boy of 13 by his actor parents in 1793. Acting, dancing, painting, promoting, and managing came as naturally as breathing. He may have come to the colonel's attention as early as 1802 when he advertised in the *Winchester Gazette* for pupils in dance and drawing and offered likenesses in miniature. After an injury he gave up dancing and concentrated on painting—anything from stage scenery or portraits to huge historical canvases like "Bonaparte Crossing the Alps." For a time he owned a racetrack. In 1812 the *Virginia Patriot* advertised his portraits in oils, and the call must have come from Carter Hall. But it was his talents as a promoter that made his name. He was the founder of the first Museum of Art and Science, which brought culture to Richmond.

Charles Bird King was one of his painter-friends who got a prospectus in 1816. The museum opened in 1817 and ran for nearly 20 years before it was forced to close for lack of money.

The rediscovery of the Warrell miniature was a victory for family tradition so far as the identity of the sitter in the ancestral portrait was concerned. But it also stimulated two other interesting questions.

Who took the initiative in hiring a painter of miniatures at this late date in the colonel's career? It was most unlikely to have been his own idea. Whatever energy he had left in those last two years was absorbed by estate planning for the benefit of his family. His eldest son, Carter, whose personality is a mystery, may have urged his father to follow his own example, but he was living at Carter's Grove. The real mover was more likely to have been Lucy, who would survive her husband for many years, with no likeness to cherish except the funereal black silhouette now in the Wallace Gallery. How much more forehanded her brother Mann Page III had been!

If she needed more examples, there was her husband's cousin and namesake, Major Nathaniel Burwell, the staff officer in the continental army who had died in 1802, leaving his widow Martha Digges to live even longer than Lucy—but not without the consolation of a miniature.

MUST WE NOT also ask, does the case for Charles Bird King as the artist engaged by the family to copy the miniature, deserve a second look? It would seem rash to rule him out, in view of the expert's proneness to error in judgments based on style and period, but it will probably take explicit contemporary evidence to rule him in. Best of all would be the scribbled signature still preserved on the stretchers of some of King's portraits at the Redwood Library (as in his portrait of Patrick Henry), but not to be hoped for here. Next might be a bill from King similar to the one we found in the papers of G. H. Burwell I from the artist Henry Beebee, in the 1850s, for the charming portrait of the patron's four children, with a glimpse of Carter Hall through the trees, which hangs today at Saratoga.

The eager searcher for these thrills should remember that though any one of the colonel's elder sons and executors—Philip, Nathaniel, and Lewis—might have served as the patron, the strongest candidate is his youngest son, George Harrison, the enthusiastic bidder for Carter Hall, the daily companion of Lucy until her death in 1843, and the friend of architects and painters as well as horse breeders. He could easily have met King in the Washington home of Dr. William Thornton, architect of the Capitol, whom King painted, and who is thought to have suggested the elegant portico for Carter Hall; or, for that matter, in King's own house and gallery on 12th Street, a center for fashionable Washington for more than 40 years.

Even if family tradition about the artist is never upheld, we can hopefully look forward to the remission of a death sentence that has prevented visitors to Carter's Grove from having any real idea of what its last great Burwell owner looked like.

BURWELL'S MILL ON THE
ROAD TO INDEPENDENCE

This article appeared in the Autumn 1986 issue of Colonial Williamsburg *journal.*

THE FIRST CLUE to the existence of the mill at the beaver dam on the road to Yorktown was found across the Blue Ridge Mountains 200 miles away. It all began in March 1980, when Mary Simpson and I drove from Williamsburg to spend a weekend with Dick and Helen Byrd at "Rosemont," Berryville, on our way back to Rhode Island. No thought of a mill that might have done the milling for Carter's Grove had entered our heads; but we were planning to visit the Burwell-Morgan Mill in Millwood, Clarke County, that

Nathaniel Burwell had built in 1785 with his partner, Daniel Morgan, the wartime hero. We would also look at Carter Hall, the great house with the mountain view to which Nathaniel Burwell moved when he left the James River in 1800.

Dick Byrd was a fellow trustee at Colonial Williamsburg. Helen Byrd had been the leading spirit in the restoration of the Burwell-Morgan Mill by the Clarke County Historical Association. After a day of splendid sight-seeing, Helen was asked if she had found any old mill books connected with her mill, although we knew how rare such books were for that period. She said, "Yes, and you'll never guess how we got them." They had been found hidden in the chimney of an old house near Millwood called "Saratoga," which Daniel Morgan had built for himself and which Nathaniel Burwell, Jr., had bought after Morgan's death.

ONE MANUSCRIPT was a mill day book, a chronological record of all the produce that either entered or left the mill during the four years from 1775 to 1778. The other was a mill ledger for the same years made up of individual accounts to which the daily entries were transferred—accounts for customers, for Nathaniel Burwell himself, and for the mill to show its annual profit. The covers of each book had been lost and with them any title or owner's name. Helen brought them from the family safe to the fireside where the four of us poured over them.

Though the paper was yellow with age and the handwriting crabbed, our eyes were soon caught by references to "Grove" or "Carter's Grove" or "30 bushels of wheat from Carter's Grove" or "10 barrels of corn from Mr. Trebell." Why were Nathaniel Burwell and William Trebell, who owned the landing just next to Carter's Grove, sending grain from the Tidewater to be milled at Millwood? It would take a wagon a whole week to get there! Then light dawned. The books had nothing to do with a Burwell-Morgan mill near Carter Hall but everything to do with a mill that Burwell must have owned at Carter's Grove.

Familiar names in the Historic Area jumped out at us. Edward Charlton the wigmaker, James Anderson the blacksmith, Alexander Craig the leather worker, James Southall who ran the Raleigh Tavern, Jane Vobe from the King's Arms, and Catherine Campbell, who was probably Christiana Campbell by another name, were all there. So was Nathaniel's brother-in-law Thomas Nelson, who would sign the Declaration of Independence, and John Randolph, the loyalist Attorney General who would not. All of them were getting their cornmeal and hominy from Burwell's Mill in 1775.

We reeled to bed at 3:00 a.m., dizzy with barrels and bushels and pecks, resolved to discover at the next meeting of the board of trustees in April what Colonial Williamsburg knew about this highly patronized watermill at Carter's Grove. I had been visiting Williamsburg almost annually for 25 years and had never heard of such a mill.

The trustees assembled as usual on a Thursday, and we had time to make a few inquiries. It would be false to say that in all the catacombs of buried knowledge that underpin a great institution of research like Colonial Williamsburg not a casket could be found containing a reference to Burwell's Mill. Specialists had seen the name on maps of the Revolutionary and Civil wars. One specialist knew of xerographic copies of these very millbooks that had been made by the State Library for the Clarke County Historical Association. However, there was no copy of the millbooks at Williamsburg; no map had carried the name Burwell's Mill since 1862; no one knew when the mill had disappeared or if its site was inside or outside the U. S. Naval Weapons Station. The fact that there ever had been such a mill came as a total surprise to the Foundation's officers.

Friday was filled with committee meetings. We decided that the time to look for the site would be on Saturday between the board meeting in the morning and the trustees' dinner that night at Carter's Grove. Our guide was William Williams, the Foundation driver, who had met us at the airport with a smile like a burst of sunshine. On the way in from Richmond, as we talked about our mission, he explained that as a boy he had played all over the woods where the mill must have been located without ever hearing of a mill site.

First U. S. survey, in 1818, of the Virginia peninsula traces Washington's routes to Yorktown. Although not a good historical map, it helped the authors locate the site of Burwell's Mill.

FROM HENRY P. JOHNSTON, *THE YORKTOWN CAMPAIGN*, HARPER BROTHERS 1881

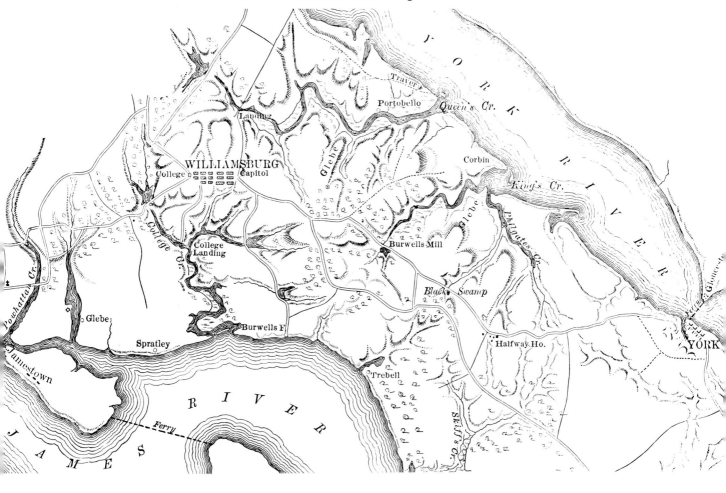

However, he knew an old Mr. Bingley who had kept a store down there, and a young Mr. Bingley who had bought some land for shooting squirrels until plumper game turned up.

Williams drove us from the Williamsburg Inn up Francis Street and turned east down Penniman Road along the spine of the peninsula. This was where the old road to Yorktown had run, down which Washington and Rochambeau had marched their troops on that hot Sunday morning in September 1781. We went under Route 64 and turned sharp right into a new cut the highway engineers had called "Old York Road" when they carved out the intersection of Route 199 with Route 64. We later figured, with the help of Williams, that they had driven this so-called "Old York Road" right through the middle of the Richard Whittaker homestead and family graveyard that had replaced Burwell's Mill Quarter on the eve of the Civil War. Our pavement crossed Route 199 and then ended abruptly in an unsightly dump where we parked the automobile, hoping that all the unseen hunters who were shooting squirrels or tin cans would miss it.

LED BY WILLIAMS, we walked to the far side of the dump, where a sunken path descended into a dense, deserted wood. We were back in the 18th century. The path curled lazily downhill for half a mile until it petered out at King's Creek. On the far side of the creek, where the road had run up the hill on its way to Yorktown, was the eight-foot metal fence of the Naval Weapons Reserve. But there was nothing to suggest a mill that we could see.

Pressed for time, we returned to the car and drove back along Penniman Road. Who should be on the sidewalk outside his home but old Mr. Bingley? We stopped, and Williams introduced us. "Did you ever hear of a watermill on that land your son and his friends bought?" we asked. "Of course," he said, "the tip of the millstone used to stick out of the ground down there, just by the left-hand side of the path." His memory went back to 1917, when he had driven down this dirt road to Yorktown in a Model T Ford to see the Atlantic fleet.

We fairly pushed him into the car, hurried back to the dump, and hustled down to the brook. We never found the millstone, but his word was good enough for us. He looked at the hole in the ground on the left-hand side of the road that once held the millhouse, at the shallow depression on the opposite side marking the millrace, and at the remains of an earthen dam winding off to the right for almost 300 yards until it reached the high ground on the other side of the brook beneath the metal fence. "Obviously," he said, "this was the mill site."

We were late for the trustees' dinner at Carter's Grove, but happy. "Just think," we said to ourselves as we scrambled to a table glittering with crystal and silver, "a few hours ago only God knew where Nathaniel Burwell got his grits."

From then on, as opportunity offered, there were three lines of investigation. First, how many mills had there been on this site, and who had owned them? An old mill that changes its name with each owner has more aliases than a criminal, but it can fall into decay and be either partly or wholly rebuilt. From time immemorial there had been a beaver dam at the head of King's Creek. The first landowner to dam the creek and build a mill on this site was Colonel Philip Lightfoot of Yorktown. That was in the 1720s when Carter Burwell was still a boy. The home farm of the future Carter's Grove Plantation was still owned by Carter's grandfather, Robert "King" Carter, and young Carter's aunt, the widowed Mary Armistead Burwell of King's Creek plantation, was married to Colonel Lightfoot. By the 1740s the first mill had broken down, and Carter Burwell, now established at Carter's Grove, rebuilt it. It was still a plantation mill, doing some extra business by the side of the York Road.

The third owner, and the first we know a great deal about, was Carter's bright son Nathaniel, who had ridden past the mill every time he went from Yorktown—where he was living with his guardian, William Nelson—to the grammar school of the college. Every Virginia planter who could afford it was improving his family mill. Nathaniel made his plans while he was still a student. He ordered two sets of millstones from England, built a brick kiln on the spot, hired a millwright and a miller, and started business in January 1775, when our mill ledger opened. The new Burwell's Mill stayed in the family until Thomas Hugh Nelson Burwell sold out in 1835.

Passing through three short-lived ownerships, it was called, in turn, Edloe's Mill, Jones's Mill, and Robert Saunders's Mill. The mill's last owner was Richard Whittaker. Though the great days of Williamsburg, when Nathaniel had sold his flour to the bakers, were long since over, the Whittakers—who had built themselves a substantial frame house where a Burwell overseer had managed a quarter—might have run a country mill for several decades if they had not been ruined by the Civil War.

T HE MILL WHEEL turned for the last time in the early 1860s. The efforts of courthouse lawyers in Yorktown to sell the mill lot on behalf of the minor heirs dragged on until 1890, when a buyer sued for the recovery of his down payment on the grounds that the huge millpond, long since dried out after the dam was breached, had been claimed by the local landowners. The mill site, picked clean in a few years, disappeared under the forest leaves while the creek was left to the beavers.

The second area of investigation was to identify the buildings, once part of the mill lot, that might be traced through excavation. The search for owners had been a wearisome toil through courthouse deeds, lightened only by depositions of 1890 in which witnesses described the mill as they remembered it. The search for former buildings was brightened by the cartographic records of the Revolutionary and Civil wars, in which buildings were often pinpointed. An even bigger excitement was Helen's discovery in the Alderman Library at the University of Virginia of an inventory of all the buildings attached to Carter's Grove plantation that Nathaniel Burwell had made for tax purposes in 1798.

There was a two-story brick millhouse, 40' x 20', on the north side of the road, with two sets of millstones, one for wheat and the other for corn. Water was delivered from the pond through a headrace to the south side of the road. Whether it then passed through a culvert under the road or ran over it could only be determined by excavation.

A tailrace on the north side returned the water to King's Creek below the road bridge a hundred yards or so east of the mill. Very close to the mill house was the two-story house for the miller, also of brick. The depositions of 1890 referred to a dilapidated mill house, a decayed miller's house with a squatter in it, and a little garden between. Williams spotted the remnants of this garden on a March day from a few green shoots of daffodils among the dead leaves. We scratched and found broken brick.

Above the sunken road—deepened today by three centuries of erosion—is a high, flat plateau on the south side. A barn must have been here and facilities for fattening and salting pork. There were references to a "shop," possibly for coopers, and a distillery. This was a real innovation for a Tide-

IVOR NOËL HUME

water plantation where the traditional spirits were rum and brandy. Whiskey was mountain dew distilled by Nathaniel's Scotch-Irish farmers on the Shenandoah quarters after he ordered his first set of stills in 1776 and then wagoned the spirits down to Williamsburg. It was sold both from Burwell's Mill and the store at Carter's Grove. It must have been sometime after the war before he added the distillery to his mill on the York Road. A lease of 1810 itemized its equipment.

In April 1982, Foundation archaeologist Ivor Noël Hume was good enough to spend a day with us at the mill site. Outdoing the beavers, we dug away until we uncovered a corner of the basement of the mill house where the brick wall was two-and-a-half feet thick, before water ran in and time ran out. We found the broken neck of an 18th-century bottle and an iron weight from a set of scales. Every particle of dirt was removed from the brickwork with a clothesbrush before it was photographed, then it was all buried again until the hoped-for day of resurrection. In November 1983, the department of archaeology made a preliminary survey of the site with a view to its possible preservation.

The Historic Area has a windmill but no watermill. The windmill has no documentary history and no archaeological potential. The forest floor on the site of Burwell's Mill has never been disturbed by the plow or the bulldozer, making it doubly promising for the archaeologist. The documentation of Burwell's Mill is almost unique in Virginia history. The only other

Jubilant Alan Simpson brandishes the first find at the mill site. Excavations conducted by Foundation archaeologist Ivor Noël Hume revealed the brick undercroft (opposite) where grain was stored.

colonial mill with comparable records is George Washington's at Dogue Run near Mount Vernon. In the great days of Williamsburg as many as ten watermills were within a mile or two of the city, not one of which has been preserved or reconstructed.

OUR FINAL EFFORT was to try to envisage the lost world between Williamsburg and Yorktown as it was before the iron curtains of national defense and the concrete curtains of urban growth clanged down on its history. The three great Burwell plantations—King's Creek, Carter's Grove, and Kingsmill—once had a meeting point on the York Road. A network of paths ran between the northern and the southern routes from Williamsburg to Yorktown. An ancient trail, running from Ringfield plantation on the York River to Trebell's Landing on the James River, crossed the York Road just inside what is today the Naval Weapons Station. Burwell wagons would lumber up the hill from the mill to the crossroads, where the little Cheesecake Church stood, then turn south to Carter's Grove.

Burwell's Mill was a famous landmark in the War of Independence. It was the scene of one of the two outposts that protected Williamsburg from the forays of Banastre Tarleton's cavalry during the early days of the Yorktown campaign, the other being on the southern route where Carter's Grove was dangerously exposed. Continental troops camped at Burwell's Mill on their way to and from the siege.

George Washington's geographer marked the mill on his route cards. French engineers all included it on their victory maps, showpieces drawn during their winter quarters in Williamsburg for galleries in France. There was whiskey galore at Burwell's Mill to celebrate the British surrender. Whittaker's Mill, the same mill by another name, was a landmark in the Civil War, with Whittaker's homestead a general's headquarters.

What could be more worthy of preservation than the only unspoiled stretch of this celebrated highway? It had survived, unmarked and virtually unknown, by nothing less than a miracle—the fact that after the erection of the Naval Weapons Station in 1918 the old York Road had nowhere to go. But the inevitable sentence of destruction had only been postponed. While our researches prospered, our hearts sank. It became clearer every year that the silent world of the sunken road was coming to an end.

You can well imagine then the authors' joy when they were told that arrangements were being made by Everette H. Newman III, owner of the mill site and the surrounding land subject to development, and the Colonial Williamsburg Foundation to safeguard this inheritance. With the cooperation of a concerned community and the successors to the Newman ownership, the site of Burwell's Mill on the road to Independence may still be salvaged.

The good news had gotten to the beavers before it got to us. They are back at the dam.

WILLIAMSBURG TO YORKTOWN: TRACING THE LAST MILES OF THE AMERICAN REVOLUTION

NO BATTLE of the importance of Yorktown in world history has left the modern visitor more ignorant of how the victors ended their long journey to the battlefield. There is no problem in learning how Lord Cornwallis ended up in Yorktown, but who knows how Generals Washington, Rochambeau, and Nelson managed the last 12 miles from Williamsburg? Try finding historical markers. Look at what the modern editor makes of Washington's diary. Scan the flood of historical maps released by the bicentennial celebrations of 1776 and 1781. Talk to the thousands of volunteers from all over the Union who came to reenact the battlefield scenes after they had marched or been bused down the Colonial Parkway. From the little that these sources have to say about the real roads to independence, the allied armies might have been dropped from helicopters.

The National Park Service, with its impressive contributions over so many decades to the interpretation of the siege, might be expected to show us how the combatants got there. Its topographical map of 1981 based on surveys of an earlier anniversary in 1931, has many valuable features. It takes in on one side all the territory of the Colonial National Park from Jamestown and Williamsburg to Yorktown; has a long historical narrative; a dozen illustrations of monuments and fortifications; and two maps of the battlefield. Major Sebastian Bauman drew one of these in 1781, which was dedicated to Washington. Bauman was the only American officer, among the many Frenchmen and Englishmen, to leave a siege map. The other map is a modern reconstruction of the battlefield to show troop positions and fortifications, but

This article appeared in the Summer 1989 issue of Colonial Williamsburg *journal.*

not the central feature assigned to the Americans as their destination before they set off from Williamsburg—Munford's Bridge.

Apart from a few scraps of fossilized history like "Old Williamsburg Road" inside the U. S. Naval Weapons Station, there is no trace of the allied routes on any of these maps. The only road that rates a scenic illustration is the Colonial Parkway, begun in 1930 and finished in 1957.

MY INTEREST IN these paradoxes was first aroused in 1982 by my role in the rediscovery of Burwell's Mill, a famous landmark in the Yorktown Campaign, described in the previous chapter. Here was not only the site of the forgotten mill outside the perimeter fence of the Weapons Reserve but a totally unmarked, unspoiled, silent, sunken path down which Washington and Rochambeau had marched to Yorktown. About the same time, while I was trying to unravel the mysteries of "The Frenchman's Map of Williamsburg" by looking closely at other maps drawn by Frenchmen after the Yorktown victory, I found a manuscript map in a French château that might have much to say about the route to Yorktown that General Nelson and the Virginia militia had used. Perhaps the obstacles created by urban sprawl, suburban contortions, and the iron curtains of national security were not insuperable after all. I decided to see if the ancient tracks, which historians of Washington like Douglas Southall Freeman had given up as beyond recovery, might be identified, and if the sacred half-mile on the road to independence, outside the Weapons Station, could be saved for posterity.

With one striking exception, there was little help to be had from contemporary journals. The meager entry in Washington's diary is misleading in itself and made more so by imperfect editing. He writes as if the rendezvous between the Continental army and the militia was not to take place until Munford's Bridge; and his editor puts the bridge on the wrong river, Skiffes Creek instead of the Warwick River.

The exception is the journal of St. George Tucker, a local resident and a colonel in the Virginia militia, whose longer paragraph about the approaches not only embodied the basic concept of two separate routes joining up before the battlefield but also mentioned specific features by name that are nowhere else recorded.

However, the real journals of the Yorktown Campaign from our standpoint are not the diaries but the maps. When a worthy historical map of the routes is finally undertaken it will be necessary to search dozens of maps for every little clue, ranging from the earliest impressions of the combatants to the U. S. Geodetic Surveys at the beginning of this century still showing vestiges of old tracks. Here we can only mention three or four invaluable guides.

First, a wonderful reconnaissance map, rough but shrewdly annotated, must have been made with the help of local Americans for the benefit of the French after their arrival in Williamsburg in September 1781. Usually re-

Pathway of an army, this dirt road (opposite) that wends past the site of Burwell's Mill once felt the tread of American and French troops marching to Yorktown. Ironically, the historic stretch of road ended up for a time in British hands, Mecca Leisure Group PLC. The property was later acquired by Anheuser Busch.

The Berthier brothers' elegant map of Williamsburg depicts troop encampments around Williamsburg on September 26, 1781, just before the march to Yorktown. French forces were deployed near the College, Americans near the Capitol.

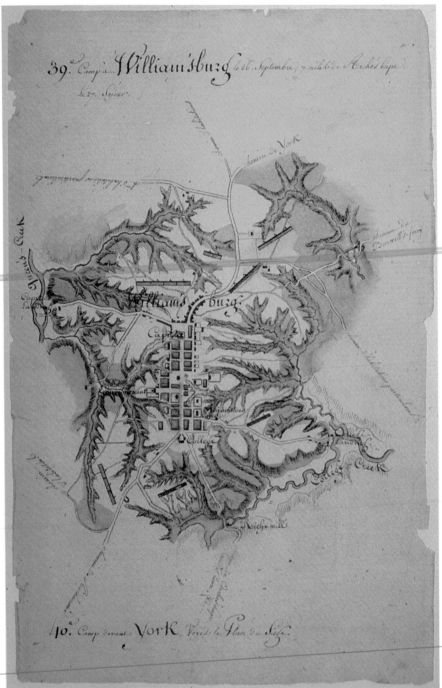

ferred to by the title of the accompanying commentary, it is called "Notes sur les Environs de York" and is Map No. 61 in Rochambeau's collection at the Library of Congress. Specialists will be grateful to the park historian Edward M. Riley, who included this key map in his edition of Tucker's journal, though he offered no commentary on just how it was related either to the special features mentioned by Tucker or to the standard U. S. maps.

Second, Washington's pathfinder, Simeon de Witt, supplied a map of the northern route from the Capitol to the west end of Main Street in

Yorktown. It is preserved today as a spidery manuscript in the New York Historical Society and was incorporated, a few years after the campaign, by Christopher Colles in the earliest survey of U. S. roads (1789). This de Witt-Colles product is like a primitive version of an AAA strip map, listing landmarks, turn-offs, and the distances between them.

Third, there is the manuscript map that I looked at closely in the Château de Gros Bois, the palace outside Paris that Napoleon gave to Alexandre Berthier after he became his chief of staff. In 1781 Berthier was the young man with the marshall's baton in his knapsack on the staff of Quartermaster General de Béville and already well known for maps of the campaign that rivaled the best work of Colonel Desandroüins, chief of the French engineers.

During his winter quarters after Yorktown, Berthier and his brother began one of the great might-have-beens of the French genius for battle maps. Desandroüins's famous map of the environs of Williamsburg, the glory of the Rochambeau collection at the Library of Congress, went no farther east than the access road to Carter's Grove. The classic siege maps of Yorktown went no farther west than the service road behind the French positions on the left of the battlefield. The only mappers, besides the Berthiers, who made anything of the lost world in between were on the staff of the Marquis de Saint Simon, but time ran out for them when they sailed back to the West Indies with Admiral de Grasse on November 4.

The Berthiers had the whole winter to complete their brilliant gallery-map of the area of today's Colonial National Historical Park, but for reasons unknown it was never finished. The section between the northern route from Burwell's Mill to Yorktown, and the coast of the James River from Trebell's Landing to the mouth of the Warwick River, is no more than a faint groundwork in pencil of roads, creeks, and homesteads looking like so many hen tracks. However, as I peered at the manuscript on the floor of Berthier's old library, it seemed much clearer than could be guessed from the one photograph ever taken. I persuaded the staff at the Bibliothèque Nationale to see if the details could not be enhanced by modern techniques.

The resulting photograph, though not ideal, threw a fascinating new light on the militia's route from the post of Colonel Edward Stevens on the outskirts of Williamsburg to Harwood's Mill on Skiffes Creek.

Lastly, we needed the best siege map for our purposes. Not one of these, whether French, British, or American, from Major Bauman's map of 1781 to the Park Service map of 1981, took in enough ground on the southwest of the battlefield to show just how the Continentals and the militia reached Munford's Bridge. But there was one that left not the slightest doubt about the location of the bridge, and of two other bridges added to it to lighten the pressure on a crucial crossing. This map was drawn by the Royal Corps of French Engineers under the leadership of Lieutenant-Colonel Querenet de la Combe, the acting chief during Desandroüins's sickness. Together with one of the two official French journals of the siege, it was on its way to France before the end of October and destined to be often copied.

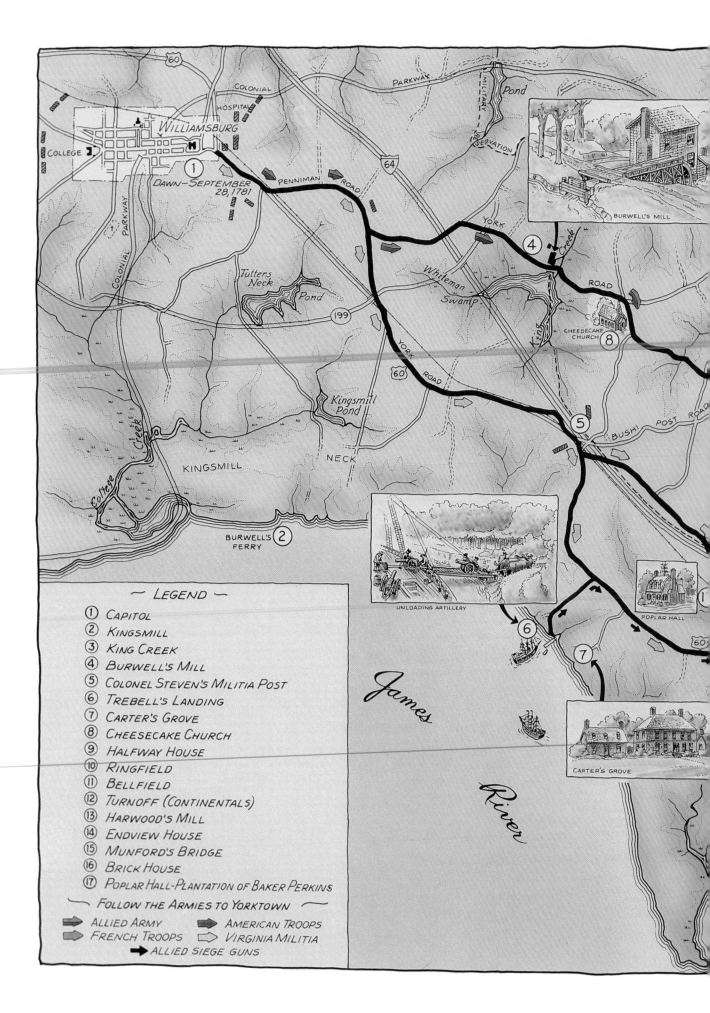

WILLIAMSBURG

COLONIAL

HOSPITAL

COLLEGE

① Dawn—September 28, 1781

PENNIMAN ROAD

Tutters Neck Pond

199

Kingsmill Pond

KINGSMILL

NECK

College Creek

BURWELL'S FERRY ②

COLONIAL PARKWAY

60

64

PARKWAY

Pond

RESERVATION

YORK

Whiteman Swamp

King Creek

ROAD

BURWELL'S MILL

CHEESECAKE CHURCH ⑧

YORK ROAD

60

BUSH POST ROAD

⑤

⑤

UNLOADING ARTILLERY

POPLAR HALL

⑥

⑦

60

James

River

CARTER'S GROVE

~ LEGEND ~

① CAPITOL
② KINGSMILL
③ KING CREEK
④ BURWELL'S MILL
⑤ COLONEL STEVEN'S MILITIA POST
⑥ TREBELL'S LANDING
⑦ CARTER'S GROVE
⑧ CHEESECAKE CHURCH
⑨ HALFWAY HOUSE
⑩ RINGFIELD
⑪ BELLFIELD
⑫ TURNOFF (CONTINENTALS)
⑬ HARWOOD'S MILL
⑭ ENDVIEW HOUSE
⑮ MUNFORD'S BRIDGE
⑯ BRICK HOUSE
⑰ POPLAR HALL-PLANTATION OF BAKER PERKINS

~ FOLLOW THE ARMIES TO YORKTOWN ~

ALLIED ARMY   AMERICAN TROOPS
FRENCH TROOPS   VIRGINIA MILITIA
ALLIED SIEGE GUNS

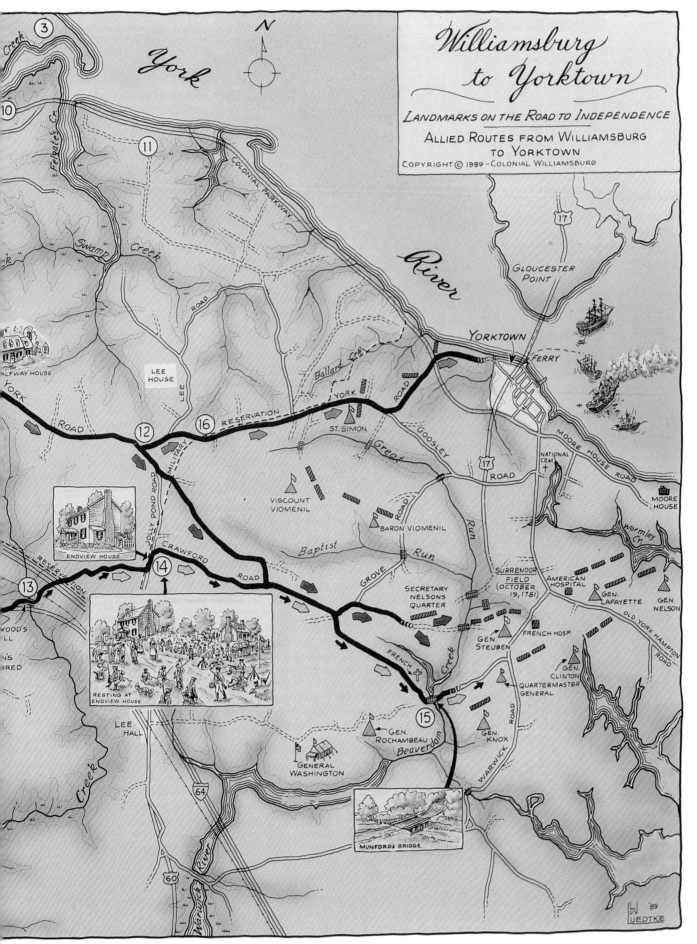

Williamsburg to Yorktown

LANDMARKS ON THE ROAD TO INDEPENDENCE

ALLIED ROUTES FROM WILLIAMSBURG TO YORKTOWN

COPYRIGHT © 1989 – COLONIAL WILLIAMSBURG

N

York River

Creek

③

⑩

⑪

COLONIAL PARKWAY

Felgate's Cr.

Swamp Creek

LEE ROAD

LEE HOUSE

HALFWAY HOUSE

YORK ROAD

⑫

⑯

RESERVATION

MILITARY

ST. SIMON

Ballard Cr.

YORK ROAD

GOOSLEY

GLOUCESTER POINT

17

YORKTOWN

FERRY

MOORE HOUSE ROAD

NATIONAL CEM

17 ROAD

MOORE HOUSE

Wormley Cr.

JOLLY POND ROAD

ENDVIEW HOUSE

VISCOUNT VIOMENIL

BARON VIOMENIL

CRAWFORD ROAD

Baptist Run

Great Run

⑭

RESTING AT ENDVIEW HOUSE

⑬

WOOD'S ...LL

...N'S ...RED

RESERVATION

SECRETARY NELSONS QUARTER

GROVE

FRENCH

Creek

SURRENDOR FIELD (OCTOBER 19, 1781)

AMERICAN HOSPITAL

GEN. LAFAYETTE

GEN. NELSON

GEN. STEUBEN

FRENCH HOSP.

OLD YORK HAMPTON ROAD

GEN. CLINTON

QUARTERMASTER GENERAL

LEE HALL

GEN. ROCHAMBEAU

Beaverdam

⑮

GEN. KNOX

WARWICK ROAD

GENERAL WASHINGTON

64

MUNFORD'S BRIDGE

60

Warwick River

Creek

LW LUEDTKE '89

MAP BY LOUIS LUEDTKE

So armed, with many unresolved uncertainties, after touring as much of the ground as we could, we embarked on our own reconstruction of the routes. The armies of Washington, Rochambeau, and General Nelson, as assembled in their campsites around Williamsburg, had prepared for a dawn start on September 18, a very hot Sunday. There were about 5,500 Continentals under Washington, 7,500 French under Rochambeau, and about 3,000 militia, mostly Virginians, under Nelson; in all some 16,000 besiegers, more than twice the besieged under Cornwallis. Not all the officers would be mounted. Light artillery would go with the columns. The heavy siege artillery, which Admiral de Barras had managed to bring down from Rhode Island, together with American artillery from the north, had arrived in the James River. There was no sign of the overdue ox teams that would drag these guns to the battlefield.

Between the Capitol and the modern intersection of Routes 64 and 199 there were no problems. The old road to Yorktown followed the line of the modern Penniman Road. The columns moved past the turnoff on the right, where the Quarterpath ran down to King's Mill and Burwell's Ferry, and on to the fork where the militia's route branched off on the same side into Martin's Hundred. The main columns, with the Continentals in the lead, continued on past a recent barracks, earmarked now as a hospital, to the point where the Penniman Road today veers off towards the Cheatham Naval Annex on the York River.

In the maps of 1781 this led to the oldest of the Burwell houses, King's Creek plantation, inherited from Nathaniel Bacon, Sr., a 17th-century president of the Council whose niece married Lewis Burwell II. Before the house burned in the 19th century, it was still famous as a place of tombs; President Bacon's tombstone was found in a field and erected in the porch of Bruton Church; the tomb of James Burwell, who died in 1718, can still be seen today in its brick enclosure near the fairway of the Navy's golf course.

It was across Penniman Road, at the edge of the great throughway intersection, that the sacred half mile of the Old York Road ran from an informal dump down to the Naval Weapons Station on King's Creek when we first discovered it. It survived, known only to squirrel hunters before developers recently moved in, because the York Road had nowhere to go after the Station erected its perimeter fence in 1918. An extraordinary graveyard of relics from the Revolutionary War and the Civil War lies buried in this half mile, either beneath the monuments of highway engineering or under the forest soil.

The site of Burwell's Mill and the outline of its great dam are here, outposts of the third Burwell plantation, Carter's Grove, that Robert "King" Carter and Lewis Burwell II had put together for the heirs of another dynastic marriage. First built by Carter Burwell, the creator of the mansion at the Grove, the mill was rebuilt by his son Nathaniel Burwell, colonel of the James City militia in the Yorktown campaign and the brother-in-law of General Thomas Nelson. An outpost for the defense of Williamsburg from Tarleton's cavalry at Yorktown had been manned here since early September by a unit of the

Pennsylvania line. Whiskey from Burwell stills on the Shenandoah River was sold here to celebrate the Yorktown victory, and in due course a distillery was added to this Burwell mill on the York road.

Burwell's Mill became Whittaker's Mill on the eve of the Civil War, and what had been Burwell's Mill Quarter, with its overseer and hands, became the site of a three-story dwelling for the Whitakers that housed Major General "Baldy" Smith in the battle of Williamsburg. The highway engineers who created the intersection of Routes 64 and 199 drove their bulldozers through the middle of the Whittaker home and graveyard. Bits of the foundations can be found on both sides of the new cut called "The Old York Road." Timber from the house, sold for a song, was used to build a two-story house on Delaware Avenue in Williamsburg. None of this history is commemorated by any kind of marker near the scene. The nearest marker, mentioning the Whittakers but not the Burwells, is on Route 60, with no real clue as to where the Whittaker house once was.

Below the mill site the old York Road peters out as it crosses King's Creek and confronts the fence of the Weapons Reserve, but the paved road ascending the hill inside continues on much the same line for almost five miles where prominent landmarks once stood, and tracks ran off through the woods to both left and right.

First came an ancient river-to-river trail of the Kiskiak or Chiskiak Indians, running from Ringfield Plantation on the York to Trebell's Landing on the James. Wagons from the mill to Carter's Grove would turn south down this road, where James Vaughan, the miller, bought a plantation shown on Desandroüins's map when he gave up milling in 1777. At the intersection on the York road, between the heads of King's Creek and Black Swamp and about five miles from the Capitol in Williamsburg, stood a little brick church. Best known as the Cheesecake Church, from the Chiskiak Indians of 1640 whom the white settlers had displaced, it was at this time a parish church of Yorkhampton, where a visiting clergyman held occasional services, a Burwell sat on the vestry, and a local farmer from the Half Way House was the clerk. Abandoned by its white parishioners in the 19th century, it was taken over by blacks and eventually razed for its bricks. All we saw on the site were traces of black graves.

N EXT CAME HALF WAY HOUSE, about six miles from Williamsburg on one side and from Yorktown on the other. A York County courthouse and an ordinary in its day, it had long been the home of the Hansfords, small planters and able craftsmen. A Hansford had been a leader in Bacon's Rebellion a century before the Revolution; another in the middle years of this century had been a blacksmith-poet. Hansford women had married into the gentry. It was not so very long since pretty Betsy Hansford,

Still visible, the old military road from Williamsburg cuts through the Naval Weapons Station (not open to the public). The millstone (upper left) at the captain's quarters possibly came from Burwell's Mill. Off the beaten path is the Lee House (upper right), built in 1641 and restored in 1915, the oldest surviving house in the region.

R. W. OSBURN, U. S. NAVAL WEAPONS STATION, YORKTOWN

urged by her 50-year-old rector to marry a rejected swain, had referred the old gentleman to Samuel XII, verse 7—"thou art the man." He duly married her and eventually moved in. This was the Reverend John Camm, professor and Tory president of William and Mary, whose bed and board at the Half Way House was better than anything he had ever known at the college. He died in 1779, leaving five children.

Two myths about the Half Way House have had a limited circulation, one that Washington and Lafayette had a two-day conference here in September to plan battlefield strategy, the other that the columns halted here for an hour to enjoy a hot Sunday dinner. Neither story has any foundation.

Farther on, a road on the left called the Lee Road runs up to Indian Field on the York River and passes the Lee House, built in Kiskiak country in 1641 by pioneer Henry Lee, and restored after the fire of 1915. Owned by nine generations of Lees—whose relationship to the Lees of Northumberland has never been demonstrated—it is easily the oldest surviving house in the region and the only survivor of the old homes in the Weapons Station.

The location of the turnoff on the right, where Washington and the Continentals headed for their rendezvous with the militia, has been the subject of much confusion. A Park Service handbook of 1957 said it was the Half Way House, a statement repeated by the Weapons Station in its house history. Washington stated in his diary that the French and the Americans separated half a mile beyond the Half Way House, but he may only have referred to the division of one column into two columns in preparation for the peel off. The DeWitt-Colles strip map suggests that the real answer was somewhat farther east.

The clues lie in a combination of the French reconnaissance map (Rochambeau No. 61) and a modern geodetic map such as the reprint of 1941. The reconnaissance map shows a track running south from the York Road, between the Half Way House and the Brick House, which it calls the Joly Pond Road. Curiously enough, there is a pond of this name today near the Powhatan Creek in James City County on the western outskirts of Williamsburg, but we have not yet discovered its derivation. The York County road on the French map joins the militia route, to which we shall soon turn, near Harwood's Mill; its destination was Mulberry Island. On the geodetic map it is roughly but unmistakably a predecessor route of today's state route 238, which runs by the side of the Weapons Reserve into Yorktown. Older residents may remember the turnoff as Halstead's Point. It was not far from the main entrance to the Station at Lackey.

Meanwhile, after the departure of the Continentals, the French continued on the old Williamsburg Road, as it is called inside the Station and continues to be so called after it emerges on what is now Route 238, until they reached a small brick house on the right-hand side about three miles from Yorktown. This must have been close to the Rising Sun Church marked on most maps today. The Marquis de Saint Simon made the Brick House his headquarters, while Rochambeau and the regiments he had brought down from the north filed off on the right to their allotted positions on the left-hand side of the battlefield. Saint Simon's own troops, which Admiral de Grasse had brought from the West Indies, marched on until they reached their positions near the river, where they could bombard both the British redoubt on the cliff and the British shipping below.

It is an ironical commentary on the limitations of historical markers that one given by the French government in 1976 to commemorate the Washington-Rochambeau route as it entered Yorktown on Route 238 was erected at a point that neither Washington nor Rochambeau ever reached. Each had peeled off earlier with his army.

The march we have just described, which had left the Capitol in Williamsburg at dawn, had reached the battlefield about four in the afternoon. Meanwhile, how had the militia fared?

Remnants of old Grove Wharf mark Trebell's Landing, where the allies' big guns were muscled ashore. Ox teams pulled them past Carter's Grove, it is believed, and "Endview" (opposite, left), where Nelson's militia rested. Near Munford's Bridge, now part of a park road, Washington and Rochambeau made their headquarters.

DAVE DOODY

Several points of interest on the southerly route call for elucidation.

First is its name. To the French cartographers it was just the other "Chemin de York." To St. George Tucker, who referred to the northerly route as "the ordinary Road to Burwell's Mill," this was "the Warwick Road from Williamsburg passing over Harwoods Mill." The English author of the French reconnaissance map also scribbled "Warwick Road to Hampton" on this road as it passed Harwood's plantation. However, before it reached this point, which was the eastern boundary of the ancient parish of Martin's Hundred as it ran along the James River from Trebell's Landing to Skiffes Creek, it would have been called the Martin's Hundred Road until far into the 19th century. It may also have been called "the back road" to Yorktown, as it often was later.

Second, what was the nature of the militia post near the entrance to Martin's Hundred, under the command of Colonel Edward Stevens of the Virginia militia?

This was the counterpart to the defensive post at Burwell's Mill; together they controlled the only two landward routes from Yorktown to Williamsburg. One French map refers to these roads as "passes" through country otherwise impassable because of woods, creeks, and marshes. If Cornwallis had chosen to break out of Yorktown instead of waiting for the relief that never came, he would have had to use either these roads or the York River.

There was also a convergence of tracks from all directions just to the east of the Stevens post. The Cheesecake Road came down from the church; the "bushie post-road" from the Half Way House; a track came up from Trebell's Landing, and there were no less than two well-traveled paths to Yorktown, which joined up again before Harwood's Mill. It was in the neighborhood of these intersecting paths that a famous tavern called French Ordinary once stood in Robert "King" Carter's day, where he might dine with assemblymen or meet his factor from Carter's Grove. Today these crucial intersections are buried inside the Weapons Station.

Third, did the militia march past the gates of Carter's Grove, the big-

DAVE DOODY

gest estate in Martin's Hundred, whose entrance today is on U. S. 60, the road to Warwick?

It would have been a stirring moment if Nathaniel Burwell, colonel of the James City militia, had been at the head of the column with his brother-in-law, General Thomas Nelson—not to mention his close friend St. George Tucker—while the colonel's lady and her numerous family watched from inside the gates. However, this scenario will not do. There is every probability that the Burwell family, like the Nelsons and Amblers from Yorktown, had been safely evacuated many weeks earlier. There is no evidence that Nathaniel was at the siege, though we would be amazed if he were not. Worse still, there is everything that Berthier's unfinished map has taught us about the uncertainties enveloping the pre-history of a route like U. S. 60. The militia may have taken the other York road through Martin's Hundred.

In our map, we have shown the alternatives. One way goes along the northern side of the western branch of Skiffes Creek; the other, passing the gates of Carter's Grove, along the southern side. The latter is much longer and therefore very unlikely.

Fourth, what do we know about Harwood's Mill? This was the landmark on Skiffes Creek mentioned by both Washington and St. George Tucker as a key feature on the militia's route. It stood at the junction of two tributaries: a northern one running almost up to the Half Way House, marked as Blows Mill Run today after the successor mill of the 19th century; and the western tributary just mentioned. The militia, on our reckoning, would have had this second tributary on their right-hand side until they crossed it to join the track that passed Carter's Grove. The mill was owned in 1781 by the prominent landowner, burgess of Warwick County, and patriot, Colonel William Harwood II. Several references to it can be found in the wartime *Virginia Gazettes*.

How does "Endview" fit into our picture? This is the one historic house of any antiquity still standing on the allied routes. It is furnished, moreover, with two intriguing historic markers.

"Endview" had been the home of the Harwoods since they moved here from their earlier house at Queens Hith about 1720. Harwoods and Curtis descendants continued to live here until it was sold to developers in 1982. A traveler from the mill turning up Route 238, alias Jolly (or Joly) Pond Road, Mulberry Island Road, etc., has a striking view of the west end of the house—hence its name—at the head of a short drive on the right-hand side. The French reconnaissance map has a symbol for the homestead and the name "Mrs. Harwood's" but not "Endview," which is recorded as its name on the roadside marker. There is also a large empty frame, built for a mural painting, with a memorial stone at its foot. Both markers record the family tradition that "Washington's troops rested here on September 28, 1781, before beginning the siege of Yorktown." The stone tablet tells the story of the faithful servant Aunt Venus, who was afraid that the soldiers would drink the spring dry until Mrs. Harwood reassured her.

We located the missing mural, whose absence was unexplained, through the courtesy of the Newport News, Va., *Daily Press*, which had commissioned it from the artist Sidney E. King for the Newport News Bicentennial of 1976. The Curtis family donated the site.

Our interest in seeing this landmark saved for posterity is almost as great as our interest in the environs of the old Burwell Mill; but when the house is, hopefully, preserved and the marker restored, it will be necessary to clarify the family tradition. It was not Washington and the Continentals, but Nelson and the militia that must have rested here.

From this point to the end of the march at Munford's Bridge, the French reconnaissance map is still our basic guide.

First came the junction of the Continentals with the militia. We saw how Washington peeled off at the Jolly Pond Road, but almost immediately his army struck off east on a line headed for the bridge that "fell into the Whitemarsh Road," to quote St. George Tucker. Crossing this now vanished road, which must have been near the head of Baptist Run, he entered the modern Crawford Road (Route 637), as it came up from the Jolly Pond Road just north of "Endview," where the militia were waiting to fall in behind.

Crawford Road, or Grove Road, soon veered north through the French half of the siege area on the west of Beaverdam Creek, the dividing line, to cross two tributaries, Baptist Run and Great Run, before joining Goosley Road on the perimeter of Cornwallis's defenses. Foolhardy advance troops that pushed too far up this road would find themselves under fire from Pigeon Hill, the British Redoubt. They would also be leaving Munford's Bridge, the crossing point of Beaverdam Creek for the American columns, far behind.

In our belief, the Continentals and the militia left Crawford Road at a point marked D on the reconnaissance map, to indicate a stretch of open country between here and point E on Beaverdam Creek, north of the bridge. It was here, we surmise, in a quarter belonging to Secretary Nelson, that elements of Tarleton's cavalry based on the other side of the Hampton Road were first spotted, and cannon brought up to send a ball or two at them across the morass. Here, too, Washington and his staff slept under the stars, finding that Munford's Bridge would have to be repaired before they could cross.

We have explained earlier that this vital bridge, although marked by name on the reconnaissance map, had escaped identification on the Park Service maps. Today the shrunken creek looks no great obstacle to an invading army, but the local surveyors of 1791 who helped the French to prepare their annotated map made it clear that the nearest ford was four miles to the south. One of the first tasks of the allied engineers, after they had established themselves in both halves of the siege area, was to add two more bridges to the north of the original one for the movement of artillery and supplies.

Helped by James Haskett, the assistant superintendent of the Park Service at the Visitor's Center in Yorktown, and by a final examination of maps that included the largest scale 1931 map in the Park Service's files, we satisfied ourselves that Munford's Bridge had been where the tour road now crosses Beaverdam Creek, just east of the headquarters of Washington and Rochambeau. We were also interested to see that dotted trails to this site, from both the Crawford Road where it veers north towards the Goosley Road and from Lee Hall further south, can be traced on the 1931 Park Service map. Troops in the rear of Washington's combined columns, such as the militia, may have proceeded more directly to the vicinity of the bridge by using one of these tracks.

ALL THAT REMAINS TO complete our reconstruction of the roads to independence is a further word about the artillery which we left on shipboard in the James River with no sign of their ox teams, when we began this story. The siege of Yorktown would not be won by infantry or cavalry, but by the big guns.

Colonel John Lamb of the American artillery wrote a letter from Trebell's Landing to General Knox on September 28, the day the march began. He explained that they had sounded the shore as far as Mulberry Island without finding a better place to land the artillery than Trebell's. But what a job it would be to get the guns up the slope there! Any visitor who walks along the cliff from Carter's Grove to the remains of Grove Wharf in the river below can see for himself. Lamb added that the *Nancy*, with the howitzers and their carriages, had just arrived the night before.

In the days that passed before the overland teams arrived on October 5, every available wagon was pressed into service, under the eyes of top brass who had come over from the battlefield six or seven miles away, including Rochambeau himself. Carter's Grove was within earshot of all this excitement, but once again the record is silent. Nor is there any tradition to tell us which way the teams went, only common sense. It seems certain that they must have taken the route past Carter's Grove. The bombardment began on October 10, and it was all over by the 19th.

THE KINGSMILL DYNASTY—
A TALE OF THREE MANSIONS

THE STORY of the Burwells of Kingsmill is full of puzzles. It deals with the rise and fall of a dynasty, itself a branch of the larger Burwell family in Virginia, which is represented by four successive heads and three great mansions and takes over a century to unfold.

One of the hallmarks of a dynasty is a lack of options when it comes to christening the eldest son. All four heads were called Lewis Burwell, like the two that preceded them and many of their successors. To tell them apart, each needs at least one other identity disk—perhaps a number, or the name of his mansion, or a descriptive epithet (like Ethelred the Unready), or a special appointment, so long as it is not just colonel. They were all colonels in the militia, except the great Lewis II, who never got higher than major.

Two Lewises had left the stage before our story began: Lewis I, the Immigrant, of Fairfield, Gloucester County; and Lewis II, of Fairfield and King's Creek, who is best remembered as the founder of all the Burwells of Virginia. The larger dynasty began with him.

In the grand dynastic plan envisaged by Lewis II and his fellow strategists in marriage alliances, a site earmarked for a future mansion was

DAVE DOODY

Kingsmill, a core tract taking its name from a pioneer, Richard Kingsmill, whose daughter Elizabeth had married Nathaniel Bacon, senior. Bacon's niece, Abigail Smith of King's Creek, after she arrived from England, became the first wife of Lewis II. Thus the Bacon alliance would contribute two seats to the Burwell family and earn the right to name more than one eldest son Nathaniel.

The Kingsmill dynasty reached its peak under Lewis Burwell III and Lewis Burwell IV, his eldest son. The father was a more creative builder than ever recognized, the son "an unlucky spender." The dynasty subdivided just as the Revolution was about to erupt. Lewis Burwell IV, accompanied by a younger son Thacker, moved out of Kingsmill to a valuable plantation on the Roanoke River in Mecklenburg County, "The Oaks." The family home on

This article appeared in the Spring 1992 issue of Colonial Williamsburg *journal.*

MARYLAND HISTORICAL SOCIETY

ATTRIBUTED TO SIR GODFREY KNELLER; VIRGINIA HISTORICAL SOCIETY

Original granite steps from Wales march up the terraced site of Kingsmill mansion (opposite), the seat Lewis Burwell built on the James in 1736. Fire destroyed it in 1844. Capped foundations and two outbuildings are preserved as a historic site in the Kingsmill residential community, developed by Anheuser-Busch. Burwell's grandson "English" Lewis Burwell V sold the plantation and moved to Richmond. Benjamin Latrobe's 1798 painting (left) shows Lewis V's new home, to the far right of the Capitol, at 12th and Cary Streets. William Byrd II (below), of Westover and Bluestone Castle, promoted the settlement of Mecklenburg County. His tract on Bluestone Creek joined Lewis IV's on Butcher's Creek.

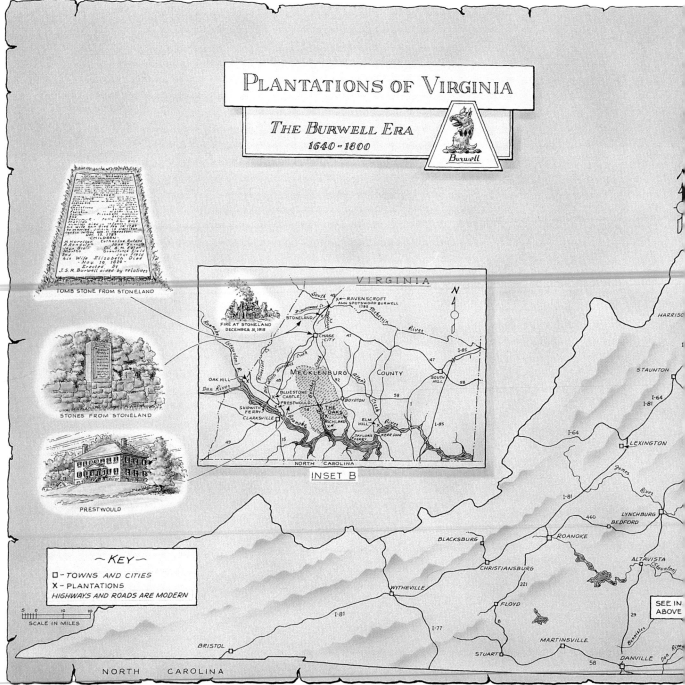

DRAWING BY LOUIS LUEDTKE

the James was given to eldest son Lewis V, an obstinate loyalist known as "English Lewis."

At about the same time a nephew of Lewis IV, yet another Lewis, whose father Armistead Burwell had spent his life as a Williamsburg merchant, also moved to an inheritance in Mecklenburg long planned for him—on the Meherrin River in the northwest corner of the new county. There Stoneland would be built. In this way, three gilded youths, Thacker, Lewis

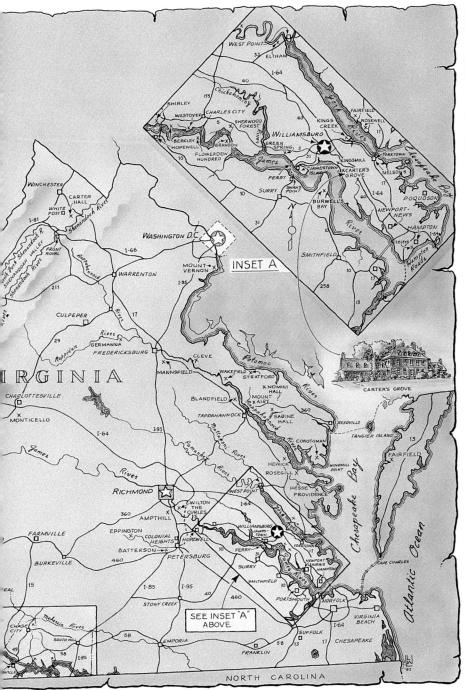

CARTER'S GROVE

Lewis Burwell III's vision of the future lay beyond his plantation on the James, Kingsmill. Sons Lewis IV and Armistead carried out his grandiose plan, planting footholds in Mecklenburg County, Virginia's "Southside," the area south of the James between Tidewater and the mountains. Inset A locates Burwell seats at Kingsmill, Carter's Grove, Burwell's Bay, Fairfield, and King's Creek. Inset B pinpoints the sites of the Oaks and Stoneland. Neighboring sites include Colonel Robert Munford's Richland; Ravenscroft, home of Ann Spotswood Burwell; and William Byrd II's hunting lodge, Bluestone Castle.

V, and cousin Lewis of Stoneland, each with an elegant bride, hoped to add two new mansions to Kingsmill if they weathered the coming war.

This vision of the future was Lewis III's, though he has never been given the credit. Builder of Kingsmill, he was the only son of Lewis II of Fairfield and King's Creek by his second wife Martha Lear Cole. Under 10 when his father died in 1710, he was brought up by his older half-brothers, Nathaniel of Fairfield and James of King's Creek, and sent to the grammar school. He was a rebellious schoolboy, and James had felt obliged to report his misconduct in a letter of 1718. Nathaniel's reply, all the evidence there is about the incident, is blistering:

> *Brother,*
>
> *I'm very much concern'd for ye occasion of your Sending & more to see how insensible Lewis is of his own Ignorance, for he can nither read as he aught to do, nor give one letter of a true shape when he writes nor spell one line of English & is altogether ignorent of Arithmetick, so that he'l be noways capable of management of his own affairs & unfit for any Gentleman's conversation, & therefore a Scandalous person & a Shame to his Relations, nor having one single qualification to recommend him; if he would but apply himself heartily one year to write well, learn ye Mathematics & Consequently arithmetick of Mr Jones, & to Translate Latin into English of Mr Ingles to learn him to spell well, I would then take him home & imploy him till he comes of Age in my Office and Plantation Affairs that he might the better be capable to manage his own, & to my knowledge this will be no disservice to him, & a greater than any other method he'l fall into through his own inclination; for my part, tis no advantage to me whether he be a Blockhead or a man of parts, were he not my Brother, but when I have to do with him, to schoole he shall go, & if he don't go till I can go over, he then Shall be forced to go whether he will or not & be made an example off (while I stand by) before ye face of ye whole College; as for y pretence of Liveing in y^e College, y^e last meeting has taken such care as will effectually provide better eating for y^e Boys, so that need not Scare him, & therefore he had better go by fare means than fowl, for go he shall, & Send him forthwith. I am,*
>
> > *Yo^r Affectio: $Broth^r$*
> > *N. Burwell*
>
> *Abington, June 13, 1718*
>   *Show him this letter*

Neither guardian would live long enough to know how their ward would turn out, James dying in 1718, Nathaniel in 1721.

No scandal seems to have marred Lewis III's introduction to married life or public life. High-flying political ambition was not his style. The dynastic ambition emphatically was, with its passion for land, slaves, fruitful marriages, and great seats.

He assured his place in Virginia history with the completion of Kingsmill and Burwell's Ferry, the riverside village from which he administered the lucrative Naval Office given to him by Governor Gooch in 1728. But it is striking how little we know about the construction of the mansion or what it cost. With the building boom on the Virginia rivers in full swing, there were models everywhere for gentlemen architects without going outside the circle of Burwell and Carter cousins. But there are no letters to or from trusted relatives or friends; no agreements with masons or master-carpenters; no invoices for imported goods; no statements of account from British merchants; not even orders for locally made bricks.

Obviously the new mansion, begun when Lewis was in his mid-20s, was both splendid and costly. Was it more than he could afford? We know that in 1736, when the building was completed, he rearranged his estate planning, as others in his class were doing, to escape from some of the rigidities of the old laws of entail. He thus could meet his expenses more efficiently and provide for younger children as well as the eldest son.

We also know that his banker was the London house of Robert Cary and Co., which would eventually—after three generations of service—force the sale of one of the family's great Mecklenburg properties to recover its investment. But that was decades away. There are no hard figures for Lewis III's financial position. However, we can figure out that in 1736 he owned between 8,000 and 9,000 acres of land—2,000 in the neighborhood of Kingsmill, another 1,800 across the river in the Isle of Wight, and 4,800 farther away in King William County. He was free to sell about 5,000 acres of this estate to meet the claims of creditors—surely a comfortable cushion.

THE CREATIVE INFLUENCE of Kingsmill on the dreams of two schoolboys who would go on to build their own seats on the James River has never been chalked up to Lewis III's credit. These boys, by a pleasant irony, were none other than Carter Burwell and Robert Carter Burwell, sons of Lewis III's old guardian Nathaniel, who became wards of the one-time blockhead and boor when Robert "King" Carter had to be replaced as their guardian after his death in 1732. Kingsmill, newly rising in all its loveliness, became home to them when they were not boarding at the grammar school.

Nor was this all. Who fixed the eyes of Lewis III's own sons, Lewis and Armistead, on the Roanoke River in Mecklenburg? Lewis and Armistead could not have thought up this future for themselves. If their father's will had survived, it would probably reflect this planning. As it is, a little study of the marriages made by the boys, and of the patents they soon took out, leaves no room for doubt.

Lewis III and his wife Elizabeth died within a year of each other, the father in September 1744, the mother in October 1745. The marriages of the boys, in the holiday season at the end of 1744, must have been planned in the father's lifetime, though only his widow lived to see the weddings. On New Year's Day, Lewis IV married Frances Thacker Bray from the mansion halfway between Kingsmill and the future Carter's Grove. She was already a widow at 23. Armistead married the 17-year-old Christian Blair, daughter of John Blair of Williamsburg, in time for their first child, the future Lewis

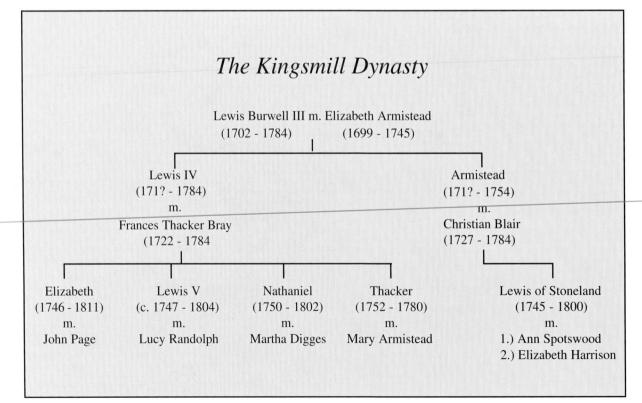

The Kingsmill Dynasty

Lewis Burwell III m. Elizabeth Armistead
(1702 - 1784)   (1699 - 1745)

Lewis IV	Armistead
(171? - 1784)	(171? - 1754)
m.	m.
Frances Thacker Bray	Christian Blair
(1722 - 1784	(1727 - 1784)

Elizabeth	Lewis V	Nathaniel	Thacker	Lewis of Stoneland
(1746 - 1811)	(c. 1747 - 1804)	(1750 - 1802)	(1752 - 1780)	(1745 - 1800)
m.	m.	m.	m.	m.
John Page	Lucy Randolph	Martha Digges	Mary Armistead	1.) Ann Spotswood
				2.) Elizabeth Harrison

Demure Lucy Randolph Burwell, wife of loyalist Lewis V, fingers an English guitar in this painting attributed to John Durand. Her brother was Speaker Peyton Randolph. She became mistress of Kingsmill after father-in-law Lewis Burwell IV moved to his son Thacker's Mecklenburg County plantation. "English" Lewis's brother Nathaniel peers from a blighted photograph of a lost miniature (opposite, left). A major in the Virginia Regiment and an original member of the Society of the Cincinnati, he was granted 5,000 acres in King William County for his military service. He died in 1802. His wife, Martha Digges, one of the legendary "belles of Williamsburg" before the Revolution, lived another 46 years. William Armistead Burwell, profiled by St. Mémin (opposite, right), was born in 1780 at The Oaks, the year his father Thacker died. He served as Thomas Jefferson's private secretary and won a seat in Congress. He was the father of William M. Burwell of Avenel.

VIRGINIA HISTORICAL SOCIETY, ABOVE AND OPPOSITE, LEFT

Burwell of Stoneland, to arrive on September 26, 1745.

About seven months after his marriage, Lewis IV took out his first patent of 4,300 acres at the mouth of Butcher's Creek, near the forks of the Roanoke. Armistead followed suit after six more months with 3,400 acres on Finneywood Creek, which flows into the south Meherrin River, now the border between Mecklenburg and Lunenburg. How could this launching of the boys into man's estate, from courtship to marriage treaties and the preemption of prime land for future seats, have been anything else but the carefully orchestrated design of the head of the Burwell household?

With equal plausibility we may guess that the prime mover in Lewis III's thinking must have been his neighbor William Byrd II of Westover and Bluestone Castle, who also died in 1744. The original surveyor of Lewis IV's tract, which abutted on Byrd's Bluestone tract, was none other than Peter Fontaine, son of the Westover chaplain of that name who accompanied Byrd on the Virginia Commission of 1728 to fix the boundary with North Carolina. So the creative builder of Kingsmill must have ended his days with a solid sense of satisfaction. He had built as fair a seat for his new line as any on the James, raised two sons to succeed him, blazed the way for more seats on the Roanoke, and set a challenging example for two of his wards.

Under Lewis IV, life at Kingsmill seemed to roll sumptuously on and on for nearly three decades. Of the three Burwell seats around Williamsburg, King's Creek was older and Carter's Grove newer, but neither got as much of the limelight. The Naval Office with its demands for hospitality, Kingsmill's reputation for fine horses, its host's love of style, and the absence of minor heirs that plagued both his Burwell neighbors, made the difference. Distinguished visitors, cousins, councillors, burgesses—and George Washington himself, who sold four carriage horses to the colonel— all expected to dine at Kingsmill and never failed to dine well.

BURWELL HEADS of households as far back as Edward, keeper of Houghton Park in England and father of Lewis the Immigrant, usually died at 40. Lewis IV, like the other exception Lewis II, would reach 60, and his lady would be with him to the end. Five children were raised to adulthood, four of whom would make elegant marriages: Elizabeth to a Page, Lewis V to a Randolph, Thacker to another Armistead, Nathaniel to a Digges. Son Armistead died at 19 in Williamsburg just before the break-up of the Kingsmill household.

Storm clouds gathered as the Revolution drew nearer. The exposure of the Robinson scandal in 1766, in which the late treasurer of the colony was found to have accommodated all his eminent friends in the "old boy net" with illegal loans, showed Lewis IV was one of his biggest borrowers to the tune of £3,000. A growing burden of debt, compounded by depressions and the needs of children as they reached the age of marriage, would plague him for the rest of his days. Added to these strains were worsening relations with Britain and memories of how divisions within the hearts of families had often spelled ruin for the great estate in the civil wars of the last century. The stubborn loyalism of English Lewis was well known on the plantation circuit long before a shot was fired.

Lewis V, a short-necked, choleric Burwell, must have earned his nickname before his father and brother Thacker decided to leave for Mecklenburg in the spring of 1775. Before the year was out a fight would break out at a Randolph dinner table in which English Lewis would call his brother-in-law Peyton Randolph, the speaker of the Assembly, a liar; and Peyton would strike the first blow. Lewis retaliated with a knife. Only the presence of the ladies restored the peace. If war came, how would it fare between English Lewis and his patriot brothers Nathaniel, the professional soldier, and Thacker, the mainstay of his father's old age?

The decision of the head of the Kingsmill family to hand over his

No representation survives of Stoneland, the most impressive house of the 1770s, which surpassed Colonel Robert Munford's Richland of the 1760s (opposite, left). Ravenscroft, or Magnolia Grove (opposite, right), was built circa 1793 by the colonel's son-in-law, John Ravenscroft, future bishop of North Carolina. Though smaller than either Stoneland or Richland, it profited from Prestwould's craftsmen.

primary seat to his eldest son, and to retire with Thacker and his new bride to his plantation in Mecklenburg, was made in the midst of the crisis created by Governor Dunmore's seizure of the gunpowder in the public magazine and his flight from the Palace to a navy ship waiting in Queen's Creek. Why Kingsmill was given up in this way at this time is hard to understand. Lewis IV had probably been living beyond his means for years, but so far as we know he was not under financial pressure from his creditors to surrender his life interest in Kingsmill.

It was not, in fact, unusual for the head of a household to hand over his seat to an eldest son who had come of age, if he had a second seat to fall back on. Nathaniel Burwell of Carter's Grove, universally admired as a good manager, would do just that in 1800, when he handed over the Grove to eldest son Carter II and moved to his ample inheritance from Robert "King" Carter on the Shenandoah River.

Lewis IV owned just as big an acreage on the Roanoke River at Butcher's Creek, where his three early patents came to between 10,000 and 11,000 acres. But whereas Nathaniel Burwell's plans for a second seat at Carter Hall had been public knowledge for a decade before he moved, nothing is known about any such planning on Lewis's part.

We can only guess that it was the marriages of two of his children—Thacker's to Mary Armistead in November 1774 and Lewis V's to Lucy Randolph in May 1775—that triggered Lewis IV's decision. Hard as it must have been to exchange all the bowing and scraping and wining and dining he was used to at Kingsmill for the rawness of the Roanoke, it might have been even harder to encourage English Lewis—the only loyalist among his children—to set up housekeeping with Lucy under the paternal roof. Besides, incurably sanguine to the last, he could always hope that Thacker might enhance the family's fortunes on Virginia's newest frontier.

Thacker quickly established himself as the head of a rising household in what had been earlier no more than a quarter, run by an overseer. He joined his first cousin Lewis of Stoneland on the Committee of Safety and was promoted to colonel while his father, a colonel at Kingsmill, became plain Lewis Burwell, Esquire, in Mecklenburg. The farm stock was in

DRAWING BY BOB SHEPPARD

VIRGINIA STATE LIBRARY AND ARCHIVES

Thacker's name. When stud fees had to be paid to Sir Peyton Skipwith, Virginia's only baronet at that time, it was Thacker who paid them.

A name for Thacker Burwell's place on the Roanoke has not been found in any contemporary document. It is called "The Oaks" because that is how two of Thacker's great-great-grandchildren, Letitia M. Burwell and Kate Burwell Boyer, raised in a later Burwell home, Avenel, in Bedford, Virginia, referred to it in a family memoir in 1883. From it we infer that Thacker and his father were buried at The Oaks, that William Armistead Burwell, Thacker's surviving son and Jefferson's private secretary, was born there, and that the whole estate was lost to the family by some combination of bad luck and negligence.

In one form or another, The Oaks was a common name for a pioneer home in a wilderness of virgin oaks, and not only in Mecklenburg. The ancestral home of William Armistead, whose line intermarried so often with the Burwells, was Oak Grove, on the East River in what is now Mathews County. It was probably his new bride, Molly Armistead, who persuaded Thacker to call their home by this name. Great Oak Plantation, Ten Oaks, and Oak Hill were in the vicinity of Chase City. Another Oak Hill was the well-known home of Major John Nelson overlooking the Roanoke River.

From clues dropped in this reminiscence, or buried in forgotten law reports, we can trace the chain of misfortunes that followed Thacker's premature death at the age of 28 in 1780 to the total disappearance of The Oaks about a generation later.

After Thacker died, Lewis IV made a desperate effort to reduce his British debt by selling off half the acreage of The Oaks while saving the other half and the mansion for Thacker's heirs. The clue to this untold story is once again Letitia. She says that a lawyer, Mr. Call, negotiated this sale and deposited the proceeds in the wartime loan office, where they were lost by the depreciation of the currency.

T HE NEXT BLOW to fall on the Burwell dynasty was the sale of Kingsmill by Lewis V, with the formal consent of his father. He had surrendered his Naval Office and his position on the bench at the outbreak of hostilities but had gone on living at the mansion. Memories of old times were occasionally revived by advertisements in the *Virginia Gazette* for his imported stallion "Regulus," which would cover mares at £25 each for the season.

His stock and his buildings suffered war damage for which he never received compensation, in spite of applications on his behalf in London after the war by his loyalist cousins among the Randolphs and the Grymeses, who vouched for his utter "Englishness." They were told that he had never resisted the rebel government of the colony.

After advertising the sale of Kingsmill with up to 2,000 acres for two years running, he got £8,500 for it in April 1783 from a speculative buyer,

John Carter Byrd. Whatever part, if any, of these proceeds was shared with his father, or his father's debtors, the sale can only have been a heavy blow to family pride. When it was built by his grandfather 50 years earlier, it was to provide a worthy seat for an indefinite succession of eldest sons. Only two had enjoyed it, and neither for as much as his own lifetime.

What are we to make of Lewis Burwell IV? His obituary in the *Virginia Gazette* for October 30, 1784, may have been less than frank, as such notices always were. Published in Richmond, to which Lewis V had retired from Kingsmill, it drew on his well-known family pride and loyalty.

> *Lately died in the county of Mecklenburg, LEWIS BURWELL, ESQ: formerly of Kingsmill, in an advanced age. It is not enough to say, that throughout the whole of his life he was distinguished by a warm affection for his family, and tenderness to his slaves; these being the duties of the first necessity. But he was also well known to be steady and sincere in his professions of friendship, unquestionable as to veracity, charitable to the distressed, sound in his understanding and, in a word, upright in his public and private conduct.*

Be that as it may, he was not a reckless gambler like William Byrd III or a wastrel like Robert Carter Burwell's son Nathaniel. His impoverished descendants spoke with awe of the luxury at Kingsmill in his day, but the mass of old bills and receipts they found in an attic of a town house in Richmond yielded no hard evidence for what his fine clothes and princely entertainment had cost him.

It was now the turn of the executors to see if they could salvage anything from this shattered estate. Other fallen lions, like Robert Carter Burwell, had left the same problems. Nathaniel "the scamp" would lose everything, including the dream mansion opposite Carter's Grove left to him. Who can withstand an unlucky throw of the dice? But the grandson Robert might still have enough, after the debts were paid, to build Long Branch on the Shenandoah.

There were four executors: the eldest son, English Lewis; a younger son, Major Nathaniel of the Virginia Regiment, who had gone back to King William County with his grant of 5,000 acres for war service; son-in-law John Page of Caroline County, husband of Elizabeth Burwell; and Lewis Burwell of Stoneland, nephew of the deceased and guardian of Thacker's children. Their duty under the will was to sell the real and personal estate for all it would fetch, apply the proceeds to the debts, and divide the balance, if any, into three shares. As Lewis V had already received his due, the beneficiaries would be Elizabeth and her heirs, Nathaniel and his, Thacker's widow and her two sons.

Letitia had been told that the British debt, with interest as well as principal, was by this date about £10,000. Family tradition at Avenel had also been critical of the executors for allowing the plantation to be sold. Why not pay off the debts from its annual production?

But who was to inspire that sort of confidence now that Thacker was gone? Moreover, the rules of the game were about to be drastically altered by the Treaty of Paris. Endless stalling of American debtors would soon be frustrated by decrees of foreclosure obtained from an American court in Richmond by British creditors. Wakelyn Welch, the surviving partner of Robert Cary and Co. in London, through his attorney Benjamin Waller in Williamsburg, could recover an original investment of about £3,000 with 18 years' accrued interest whenever he liked. The only alternative for the Burwells to the humiliation of a public auction would be a private sale.

This was the solution in the spring of 1794 when Welch got his de-

cree. A Burwell-Nelson deal was struck. Major John Nelson of Oak Hill owned a plantation about a dozen miles upriver from The Oaks. Born in 1748, a son of Secretary Thomas Nelson and a nephew of William Nelson, President of the Council, he had been raised in their "compound" on the cliffs of Yorktown. He seems to have settled in Mecklenburg about the same time as Thacker, but to have then decided, like Thacker's brother Nathaniel, to join the Virginia Regiment. Both fought at Yorktown, rose to the rank of major, and were original members of the Society of the Cincinnati. Nathaniel's wife, Martha Digges, had been more like a daughter to Secretary Nelson before the war, so there was a very special relationship between the families.

John Nelson's response to the suggestion from two of the executors, Major Nathaniel Burwell and Colonel Lewis Burwell, that he might like to buy The Oaks was positive. After a quick visit in July 1794, he waived his option to request a new survey and took over The Oaks at the end of the year. At 30 shillings an acre for more than 5,000 acres, this would yield about £7,700, of which £1,000 might be available for other creditors.

To say that all had been lost for Lewis IV except honor would be going too far. One great mansion had been lost to the family at Kingsmill, and the hopes set on a second seat at The Oaks were now forever dashed. It was even uncertain for several years whether there would be any balance left from the sale after a long line of creditors, aroused by Welch's success in the courts, had been appeased. In 1798 Nathaniel and Lewis V, against an action for debt brought by another British company, pleaded that all the assets were gone. This was only true at the time because Nelson had fallen behind on his payments; but whatever relief might turn up, it was only too clear that dynastically speaking, this branch had shot its bolt.

But all was *not* lost. Thacker's line survived. Letitia related how debts due to Thacker's estate, and only repaid after his death, made it possible for his son, William Armistead Burwell, to settle in Franklin County in 1802 after he had left William and Mary. His guardian, Lewis of Stoneland, who owned a plantation in that county, may have directed him there. This was where he lived as Jefferson's private secretary and a member of Congress, when he was not residing in Washington with his own carriage. He built no elegant seat but certainly enjoyed the life of a Virginia gentleman, as did his descendants at Avenel in Bedford before the Civil War.

No record has been found of what happened to The Oaks, with its family graveyard, after it passed to the Nelsons on Christmas Day, 1794. The Major died at Oak Hill in 1827. His son Thomas, a congressman, sold their lands on the Staunton and moved to Butcher's Creek, where he lived at Wheatlands before leaving the county altogether in the late 1830s. The aborted mansion of Lewis IV might never have existed.

Stoneland has been preserved from any such oblivion by more than one stroke of luck. First, it is remembered as the home of perhaps the most prominent county leader of Mecklenburg in the Revolutionary War. Second, the fire that destroyed the mansion and eight lives on New Year's Eve 1815 was described shortly after the tragedy by a friend of the family who was

DAVE DOODY

Seen from the air is the site of Thacker Burwell's The Oaks, surrounded by the cobalt waters of Butcher's Creek and the Roanoke River. On the east side of the creek, at the top right of the picture, lay Richland, where only Munford family tombstones remain. Sir Peyton Skipwith's Prestwould (opposite), surrounded by woodlands aglow in autumnal light and rimmed by Bugg's Island Lake, set the new standard for Southside elegance. Completed in 1795, it was constructed of stone quarried on the plantation.

also a gifted letter writer, Elizabeth Munford Kennon. Third, the tomb of Colonel Lewis Burwell in the family graveyard, together with stones from the nearby ruins, were eventually transplanted to Chase City, where they can be seen today.

To have these mementoes is much better than to have nothing at all, as at The Oaks; but each is a little mystery in itself, and the biggest mystery of all is that no one has attempted a history of the house, however modest, or tried to tell us what it looked like.

The man best able to do this in our century was the late William B. (Billy) Hill, director of the Roanoke River Museum. Hill never published anything about Stoneland, but he made the Colonel's career the subject of a talk which he gave in 1956. Little was said about the house, nothing about the Colonel's role as executor of his uncle, Lewis IV, or as guardian of Thacker's children. Highly relevant, however, were Hill's opinion of the Colonel's stature—"the best exponent of the class ideal of the English gentry in our county"—and his description of the estate surrounding his seat, taken from an advertisement in the *Virginia Gazette* of April 23, 1794.

Such advertisements are the best contemporary descriptions we have of two other Burwell seats, Kingsmill itself and Burwell's Bay; though in this case more descriptive of the plantation than of the mansion. Hill assumes the Colonel was heavily in debt to British merchants and highly sensitive to the bankruptcies of recent years, but quotes no figures and knows that no sale followed. Nor was there any sign in his own will, six years later, that the payment of his debts might bite deeply into the landed estate. The advertisement may just have reflected the almost automatic desire of a debt-conscious class to test the waters.

Colonel Lewis Burwell owned 6,000 to 7,000 acres—some of it originally intended for his brother John—in a compact estate lying on both sides of the South Meherrin River. It was well-timbered and watered by three creeks. Besides abundant meadow for stock, the land produced top quality tobacco and wheat on its three plantations. A mill at the mouth of Finneywood Creek yielded 100 barrels of corn a year in tolls. A still yielded 300 to 400 gallons of brandy from the orchards. There were good prospects of iron ore, with a site on the Meherrin for a forge and a furnace. At the center of the whole property was "a good stand for business," a store and dwelling house for a merchant, and another large house suitable for a tavern. His own house was "large and commodious." Hill adds an item from another advertisement in 1796, a plantation schoolhouse where Latin, French, English, arithmetic, and writing were taught, with board £10 to £15 a year, tuition £8 a quarter.

Just when and by whom the mansion was built the local historians have nothing to say. Armistead Burwell, who took out the original patents, is sometimes referred to as "of Stoneland," but there is no evidence that he, as distinct from his overseers, ever lived there. Raised as a merchant in Williamsburg, he served in the city government and was representing James City County as a burgess when he died in 1754 while his two sons, Lewis and John, were still children.

Lewis came of age in 1766 and married in 1768 Ann Spotswood, granddaughter of the former governor. This would have been a logical time for them to start housekeeping in Mecklenburg if there were a house ready for them. But the date of their move, and of Stoneland's construction, has never been pinned down. We can assume from the evidence of deeds, which recorded the county of residence, that the move was no earlier than January 1771, and could have been as late as December 1774. Surely by the latter date, with four children under six years old, they were already settled in Stoneland. But the earliest surviving letter from the new mansion, with its name scribbled beside the Colonel's signature, is from 1779.

In the Yorktown campaign Lewis saw little of the action that came the way of his cousin Major Nathaniel Burwell. But he commanded three battalions of militia, and afterwards could count on winning most of his electoral contests as a war hero. When he died of apoplexy in 1800 at the age of 55, his two wives—Elizabeth Harrison followed Ann Spotswood in 1789—had delivered 16 children, all but one of whom would reach adulthood and marry well. It must have looked as if a merciful providence had given the Burwells of Kingsmill another chance of dynastic glory.

All hopes for the third seat of the Burwells of Kingsmill went up in flames in 1815. It was December 31, or perhaps the early hours of the New Year, when the household went to bed. Many of the older folk, including Mrs. Burwell, were probably at other parties. A vivid account of what happened was recorded three weeks later by Elizabeth Munford Kennon in a letter to Rachel Mordecai:

> *. . . And now my Rachel, List, List, List. For I will a tale unfold, whose lightest word will harrow up thy soul. . . . Poor Mrs. Burwell, the mother of your favorite Martha, on the last night of the old year had her house burned down, and dreadful to relate, eight persons were destroyed. Her very worthy and affectionate son Henry with his wife; a child of her son Randolph; a daughter Mary of her son John Burwell; and four negro girls who slept in the house. Your justly admired pupil, showed such presence of mind, and goodness of heart and courage also; that she deserves great credit.*
>
> *It is said that the alarm was first given by a young man who was there, and who was awakened by the smoke in his room. He sprang out of bed, but found the floor so hot he could scarcely bear it with his naked feet. He however began to immediately call out, and ran to Martha's room, the door of which he burst open; the devouring element raged so violently that escape by the stairs was nearly impossible, and unfortunately the whites were all above stairs, and it caught below.*
>
> *By the time Martha was made sensible of her danger, the flames rolled on through the upper passage and came in at her door. She shut the door as a barrier against the fire and took a little negro*

girl who was in the room with her, and putting her out of the window, and reaching down as far as she could let her drop. Then she got out herself, holding by the window frame to break the fall as much as possible and called out for some person to try and catch her. A negro woman heard and ran to assist her; she then let go the window, and scraping down the side of the house, prevented herself from descending with as great rapidity as she otherwise would have done. The servant caught her, but the weight broke one of her arms, while Martha escaped without injury except wounding her hand with a nail, which perhaps was in a plank.

The young gentleman, after she got out, leaped after her, but not using her wise precaution, he was so hurt by the violence of the concussion when he struck the ground that he was taken up insensible and did not speak for several days.

What makes the catastrophe more lamentable is that Henry Burwell and his wife on the first alarm got downstairs, and could have escaped without injury; but she recollected the child, it is thought, for it had been left by its parents in their care, and ran back again though the whole place was in flames. Henry, seeing her do so, pursued her and bore her back through the dreadful conflagration, for he had barely cleared the stairs when the whole of it fell in. They did not find the child or its nurse. They came out alive, but she only lived twelve hours, and he dragged out a miserable existence of three or four days. . . .

The unfortunate old lady was from home when the accident happened. Oh, what a dreadful scene awaited her return!

E. B. Kennon

P. S. The little negro Martha put out of the window, escaped unhurt, it is said.

We can imagine the story of the fire and the funeral being told and re-told with variations for decades, especially by faithful servants of the family in the households of sons and grandsons of the Colonel living in the neighborhood. One anecdote to surface recently identifies the negro woman who broke Martha's fall down the side of the house as Fanny, heroine of the "downstairs" tradition in the family of Spotswood Burwell.

Clearly, all the business and personal records kept in the house and its connected offices would have burned. No effort was made to rebuild Stoneland, but that is not to say that everything was abandoned. Deeds and taxes testify to the continuation of Burwell ownerships, as modified by the redistribution of Henry's share. Farming must have continued. The family graveyard, with its new tombs within its enclosed wall, would receive the body of Mrs. Burwell after her death in 1824, and then, at some unrecorded date thereafter, a tomb truly worthy of an illustrious Virginian. The inscription says it was "erected by J. S. R. Burwell, aided by relatives." This must have been John Spotswood Ravenscroft Burwell, grandson of the Colonel and son of his executor Lewis Burwell.

This was much more likely to have been done before the Civil War than during Reconstruction, when the old way of life was doomed; but the evidence of the Confederate map of 1864, with such names as Colonel Burwell, marking the site of Stoneland, of Burwells Mill and Burwell Quarters on the South Meherrin River, and dwellings of a John Burwell and a Robert Burwell not far away, would suggest that neither the wilderness nor the squatter had yet taken over.

The Tobacco Planter published a letter in Boydton on Christmas Day 1869 from a correspondent using a nom de plume with Piney Wood as his address. He found it very sad that people like himself had missed their chance to build fine homes when they were able to do so. "Our idea of a fortune was two plantations and a hundred negroes, out of debt and a plenty of money." Time enough then to think of a fine house . . . but when a man's best property was taken from him, it was too late! Billy Hill guessed that this might have been Peyton Randolph Burwell, but we know from the records of a family picnic that Piney Wood was the address of J. S. R. Burwell and his son Lewis T. Burwell. Before long there would be nothing but a wilderness of piney woods. The only Burwell left in the area would be a beloved country doctor, a great-grandson of the Colonel, practicing medicine in Chase City until he retired in 1928.

D URING THIS HALF century, when genealogists, antiquarians, and historians were beginning to take Virginia's heritage more seriously, there must have been more than one visit to the mansion site. R. A. Brock published his pioneering articles on the Burwell family in the *Richmond Standard* in 1881, showing that he was familiar with the Colonel's tomb and the sword preserved by Dr. Burwell. A visit to the graveyard in 1889 by a correspondent of the *Richmond Dispatch* accompanied by the mayor of Chase City produced a basic account for the turn of the century. In the earliest version, corn was still growing on the site; in the latest, not a trace of tillage or human habitation and "scarcely a brick from the massive chimneys" could be seen. The burial ground, on a rise with a commanding view, as it was at Carter's Grove, had lost its protective walls, but many graves could be seen.

Resting against a towering elm was a slab of white marble, six feet high, three feet wide, and several inches thick, at the head of the Colonel's grave. Its inscription, beginning "Here are the ashes of a great and good man" and including the marriages of 15 of his 16 children, ended with a credit line for J. S. R. Burwell. The usual headline for this story was either "Genealogy on a Tombstone" or "Comprehensive Inscription of a Hero and His Family."

When the earliest Burwell tombs from Fairfield were transplanted to the churchyard at Abingdon in 1911, a faithful account of this rescue was published. Typical of our mystery is the absence of any explanation of how, or when, the Colonel's tomb came to be embedded in the grass outside St. John's Episcopal Church in Chase City, which has no graveyard. As the successor church to the "Old Church" that the Stoneland and Ravenscroft Burwells did so much to support in their day, this was defensible; a sanctuary was found for a monument that would otherwise have perished. But an opportunity was lost to learn more about how things once had been at Stoneland by ensuring that the condition of the ruins at this time was fully recorded.

A clue may be found in the role of the Hudgins family in Chase City, where Chief Justice Edward W. Hudgins built his residence in 1928 with its five-acre garden, MacCallum More. Stones removed from Stoneland were used to ornament the garden wall; the house was preserved as a museum; and in 1984 a Lewis Burwell Day was proclaimed throughout the state by Governor Charles Robb. A bronze tablet on the garden wall, honoring the old war hero of two centuries ago, was unveiled by six-year-old Kriston Kirk, a descendant, in the presence of Mrs. Lewis Burwell Puller, widow of Marine hero Colonel "Chesty" Puller, of World War II and Korean War fame. Nothing, however, was added to our knowledge of historic Stoneland.

Was it a grand house, or only a big house? Nothing is known about the interior woodwork in spite of the claim made for the mantel in the MacCallum More museum. Nothing definite has emerged about the outside of the house, though the name "Stoneland" continues to intrigue. Prestwould was made wholly of stone, quarried on the estate, cut into blocks, and laid by stonemason Jacob Shelor. Ravenscroft, built by the Colonel's son-in-law about the same time, has stonework in its basement and on its chimneys resembling the work of Shelor. The odds seem to favor a big frame house, like Richland. Martha Burwell, who scraped down the side of the house when she dropped from an upstairs window would have known, but Elizabeth Kennon only mentions the nail that might have cut her hand.

W HAT ELSE may be uncovered? If some of the typical clues in the search for lost mansions have not turned up, such as an inventory specifying rooms or an insurance policy with a rough sketch, we have no doubt that others will surface. A search for foundations in those piney woods, of the kind that exposed misconceptions about the first Burwell mansion at Fairfield, would not be prohibitively expensive. The editing of the Skipwith Papers, currently in progress at the College of William and Mary, might reveal something. But it is the prodigious progeny of the Colonel and his two ladies that offers the best hope for information retrieval. In our search for the missing miniature of Colonel Nathaniel Burwell of Carter's Grove and Carter Hall, lost to the learned world of our century for over 60 years, we found it had not been lost at all, only borrowed within the family.

If The Oaks is still a target for an aggressive "lost and found" department, how much more promising must Stoneland be?

COLONIAL CRICKETERS: YOUNG MILORDS ENJOYING THEIR ENGLISH SCHOOLDAYS

HOW CRICKET BEGAN in human history is a matter for conjecture. We can feel fairly sure that, once *homo sapiens* was comfortably descended from the trees and romping around upright on fairly level ground, it was only a matter of time before he invented half a dozen ball games. Handy sticks were everywhere. Man-made balls of stitched leather replaced the less durable balls in nature. The men were separated from the boys when the future of these primitive ball games still hung in the balance. A vigorous game like cricket, combining team spirit with individual prowess and frequent casualties, found its rightful place, we assume, among the sports of warring tribes. When bets were made and liquor flowed, inspired bards must have sung of aboriginal Waterloos won on the playing fields of grounded apes.

What is not conjectural is the emergence of cricket in a corner of England, once wooded, lying between the south and north downs, called the Weald. For centuries before the invention of printing, it was played on village greens here by the lord of the manor and his tenants, with the music of bat and ball and the murmurs of approbation soothing some of the sores of serfdom. The preindustrial cricket bat, curved like a hockey stick, can show up in the stained glass of a medieval cathedral window or the margin of an illuminated manuscript. It is not until the end of the 16th century that recorded references to the game begin to surface, though they may carry us back further than that, being perhaps a deposition that one witness, all of 60 years old, played cricket with his schoolmates, or that his family had manufactured cricket balls since the reign of King Henry VIII. Those counties of the Weald, like Kent, Surrey, Sussex, and Hampshire, were to be the seed-

Benjamin West, a fellow colonial and a future president of the Royal Academy, was only a few years older than his subjects when he painted almost identical versions of "The Cricketers" in 1763 and 1764. No other artist has caught the spirit of the young milord during his English schooldays with such brilliance.

The figure at the extreme right, believed to be Arthur Middleton, a future signer of the Declaration of Independence, was painted *without* the sword in the version of 1764. Why? Possibly because the artist had been told that a sword was too dressy for a cricket match. None of the others was wearing one.

beds of modern cricket.

The watershed between a game played from time immemorial by vil-
lagers and schoolboys and the "big cricket" of high society and high stakes
was about 1700, with some anticipations of the new age as early as the Restoration of Charles II in 1660. At least two ducal offspring of Charles II's
mistresses, and all the Hanoverian kings and their offspring from George II
to George IV, were enthusiasts for big cricket. George III's father, "poor Fred,"
the Prince of Wales, was thought by many of his friends to have died in 1751
from the effects of a cricket ball that struck him in the chest; but this did not
discourage George III from warmly exhorting his own children to "Play up,
play up, and play the game!"

Colonel Banastre Tarleton, an enthusiastic promoter of big cricket in
England, seems to have rattled his saber in more than one contest: "During
the cricket match between the Duke of York and Colonel Tarleton, a smart
altercation ensued respecting the game that had nearly put an end to it!"

THE CENTERS OF big cricket included Hampton Court, where the
London and Surrey teams were entertained in 1723, and the royal house at
Kew where George III's children were initiated. Great country houses like
Knole in Kent or Goodwood in Sussex were bywords for lavish patronage
and stellar performances at the wicket from generation to generation. The
third Duke of Dorset of Knole, as handsome a figure as Gainsborough ever
painted, was said to spend a thousand pounds a year on a stable of cricketers,
and vastly more on his mistresses, as we might guess from the companion
portrait of his favorite, *la Baccelli*, done by Gainsborough in the same year
as his own, 1782. The Dukes of Richmond lived like royalty at Goodwood
near Chichester. It was the fourth Duke whose cricket match Wellington's
officers joined on the eve of the battle of Waterloo, and whose Duchess gave
the famous ball that night in Brussels.

In London itself four fashionable clubs laid down in turn the laws of
cricket between the 1740s and the end of the century; the earliest at the Artillery Ground in Finsbury, where a ticket for the match of London versus Kent
in 1744, which was opened for Kent by a Duke of Dorset, was sold for two
shillings and sixpence, and is now a museum piece; the second at the Star
and Garter Club in Pall Mall; the third at the club in White Conduit Street;
and the fourth the Mary-le-Bone Cricket Club (M. C. C.), founded in 1787
by Thomas Lord, to be known as Lord's, the most famous cricket ground in
the world.

A sport already so blessed when George III came to the throne in
1760 must have been known to almost every English schoolboy, whether he
went to a great school like Eton, Harrow, or Westminster, or to a local grammar school or a little private academy. Sons of wealthy planters in Virginia
or South Carolina, sent to English schools, must have run into cricket when

they got there, if they had not already batted a ball around on their own plantations. William Byrd II must have seen it at Felstead School in Essex; Thomas Nelson of Yorktown in his fashionable academy at Hackney; John Carter of Corotoman and Shirley when he attended a private academy on the edge of Stepney Green. Lewis Burwell of Fairfield, future president of the Council of Virginia, assuredly saw cricket on the College Field at Eton when he was there in the 1720s. A recent Etonian had written a Latin poem about the game in 1706, which ranks today as an original source for its rules at that time. Titled old Etonians were prominent in all the London clubs mentioned.

The layout of the game in the early years of big cricket was admirably depicted in a famous painting of the mid-'40s, now at Lord's, by Francis Hayman, when the laws of cricket were first codified to meet the new demands. So popular was Hayman's work, it was repeatedly copied by other painters, or engravers, or even embroidered on a linen handkerchief by a lady admirer. Entitled "Cricket as Played in the Mary-le-Bone Fields," this description is retrospective inasmuch as it was painted by Hayman more than 40 years before the M. C. C. was established.

THERE ARE 11 players on each side. The wickets at either end of the pitch, which is 22 yards long, are of two stumps, with the single bail resting on their forked tops. A batsman is out if the bail is dislodged; a third stump will be added later to meet the bowler's complaint that his fast ball can pass between the stumps without disturbing the bail. The curved bats of the batsmen, and of the two umpires who carry a bat as a badge of office, are traditional, to be replaced later in the century by the modern straight bat. Behind the batsman's wicket is the wicketkeeper. The bowler at the other end is about to deliver an under-arm ball. The fielders do not wear gloves, thus depriving their modern successors of the pyrotechnic miracles performed by fielders in baseball. In the foreground are two scorekeepers to notch on their sticks the runs scored by the batsmen. A ball struck out of the cricket ground that never touches the field has been "hit for a six"; otherwise, four. Experts in every wrinkle of the game at this time vouch for Hayman's accuracy.

The real expert in cricket, which eventually becomes for many Englishmen as much a religion as a sport, is as quick to detect an error as if he were a bishop presiding over the administration of the sacraments. But this is only true of big cricket in England. On the plantation circuit in Virginia, the Byrds, Burwells, Carters, Harrisons, and Wormeleys, if we may guess from the example of Westover, enjoyed the game as a spur-of-the-moment recreation, to be offered their guests like billiards or shooting with bows and arrows. Its grander moments, as the sport of kings and dukes, which ladies might enjoy either by practicing with their brothers or organizing clubs and matches for their own sex, would be no more than hearsay for most planters in the colonies. A woman living in England, practicing with her brothers, is credited with having invented round-arm bowling at the end of the century to avoid the nuisance of entangling the ball in her own voluminous skirts.

Benjamin West came from a Quaker home in rural Pennsylvania that was unlikely to have seen much cricket. His father kept an inn on what is now the campus of Swarthmore College; his mother was a second wife whose tenth child, born in 1738, was Benjamin. He had no formal education to speak of, either in reading and writing, or in painting, which caught his imagination when he was a boy of nine and totally absorbed him. Inventive spirits like Robert Fulton, the engineer, and William Henry, the gunsmith, who knew him in his youth, recognized his quality, as did two farsighted patrons in Philadelphia. One of these was the Reverend William Smith, a college president of the future University of Pennsylvania; the other, William Allen, a merchant and future chief justice. West, a quick learner and hard worker, always made the most of his opportunities.

When Smith and Allen and a visiting artist like John Wollaston had done what they could for him, he sailed to Europe in 1760, in one of Allen's ships, for the experience that would change his life—three years' study among the painters and paintings of Italy, France, and England. On board with him was Allen's eldest son John, whose portrait he would paint in Italy. Two more sons, James and Andrew, due to arrive in England for their legal education before too long, would offer more subjects. Meanwhile, there were copies to

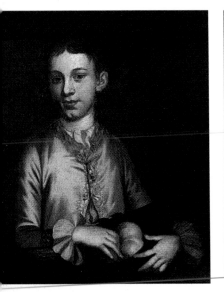

DAVE DOODY

Rosegill on the Rappahannock was the ancestral home of the Wormeleys. Earlier Wormeleys, like earlier Burwells in the 18th century, had been grandchildren and wards of Robert "King" Carter. Nearest neighbors were the Grymes family at Brandon, where Carter Burwell had married Lucy Grymes and his son Nathaniel, Sukey Grymes. Modern occupants of Rosegill, Charles and Polly Longsworth, stand where colonial cricketers in the Burwell cousinhood might have tested their skills.

FROM *LE KEUX'S ENGRAVINGS OF VICTORIAN CAMBRIDGE*, CAMBRIDGE UNIVERSITY PRESS

Three of the five cricketers attended Trinity Hall (left), shown here in its Victorian dress from the gardens at the back. Ralph Wormeley (opposite, left) was ten when John Wollaston painted him before he left home for Eton College. At 18 (opposite, right) he is painted by Robert Edge Pine in the gown of a Fellow Commoner of Trinity Hall. The building in the background is almost certainly Clare College and not Trinity Hall.

be made of old masters for the collections of Mr. Allen and his circle, and every imaginable lesson to be learned from both the quick and the dead. He reached England in August 1763, preceded by excellent reports of his progress, and set off almost at once for a month's visit to Bath, where Mr. Allen was staying, with side trips to showplaces like Oxford University, Blenheim Palace, and the Earl of Pembroke's seat at Wilton. His friendship with Gainsborough may have begun at Bath; with Reynolds, on his return to London if not earlier.

The English visit was expected to be short, because his three years were up and he had a fiancée in Philadelphia impatient to see him. But how could he possibly go back to a married life in Pennsylvania after all the in-

An 18th-century cricket match played in London's Regent Park area springs to life in Francis Hayman's panoramic study. It was painted about 1744.

toxications of old masters and new masters and rumors of patrons who might even include the king of England? The success of his first exhibition in the spring of 1764, at the Society of Artists in London, with three paintings suggested by Reynolds, made up his mind. Smith and Allen, who happened to be in London at the time, approved. His widowed father brought his fiancée over to London for a September wedding, and the happy groom never crossed the ocean again.

"The Cricketers" was one of his very earliest paintings in England. He could hardly have settled down to a professional life in London before mid-October, and it must have been finished, or at the very least well advanced, before one of his five subjects, Arthur Middleton, left for home in December 1763. West himself was no more than 25. If no thought was given to including "The Cricketers" in his first exhibition, that could only have been because its subjects were unknown to fashionable London. Its popularity with its American sitters and their families is sufficiently attested by an immediate request from the Izard family for an identical copy which West signed and dated London 1764. His studio at this time was near Covent Garden.

The choice of the cricket theme needs no explanation. All sorts of enchanting variations of "Boy with Bat" were already part of the grand-manner tradition in English portraiture. West may very well have seen one of the grandest examples at Blenheim, in Thomas Hudson's "Family of the Duke of Marlborough," which has two such youths with their bats on the fringe of the group. There was probably no thriving studio in London which did not include a cricket bat, a ball, and a wicket among its props.

There are, however, two puzzles that require an explanation. First, there is the identity problem. Who exactly were these five young men, and where were they when the artist painted them in the fall of 1763? Four different explanations have made their way into print, two of them derived from the family traditions of the Allens or the Izards, who commissioned the original versions, and two from modern historians of either art or cricket who have reached their own judgments on the basis of the evidence.

Of course there is common ground in their divergent views. It is agreed with only one dissenting voice that all five were students born in America and eventually sent to the mother country to complete their education: two sons of Judge Allen, James and Andrew, from Pennsylvania; two members of prominent families in South Carolina, Ralph Izard and Arthur Middleton; and Ralph Wormeley of similar status in Virginia. The dissenting voice would substitute an unidentified Mr. Beckford for the well-known Arthur Middleton, but as this is derived from the weaker, disrupted Izard tradition, it is discounted here. The real argument to be met, if the babble of discordant voices is to be reduced, is twofold: first, not who these young men were, but which was which, and second, what their educational experience had been before West painted them.

Our solution, starting from the left, is as follows:

(1) James Allen of Philadelphia, 21, younger of the two Allen sons in the portrait, graduated from the College of Philadelphia in 1759, and after

preparatory studies in law, sent to the Middle Temple in London, 1761-1765.

(2) Ralph Wormeley of Rosegill, Virginia, 18, entered Eton College at 12 in 1751, and Trinity Hall, Cambridge, in 1762, as a Fellow Commoner, where he met Ralph Izard.

(3) Andrew Allen, 23, went through exactly the same educational experience, during the same years, as his younger brother James.

(4) Ralph Izard, of Goose Creek and Charleston, South Carolina, 21, was at school in England for 12 years, first at Hackney School in the eastern suburbs of London, then at Trinity Hall, Cambridge, where he was also a Fellow Commoner. He returned December 1764 with his college friend Ralph Wormeley, who was entertained by the Izards in Charleston on his way back to Virginia. Known to have been athletic in his youth, he may even have shone at cricket.

(5) Arthur Middleton of Middleton Place, South Carolina, 21, was sent to Hackney School in 1754, entered Trinity Hall, Cambridge, in 1760, and was at the Middle Temple with the Allen brothers when the picture was painted. He left for home December 1763.

The conclusion reached here that the three cricketers educated at Cambridge University all attended the same college is based on the standard work of reference for Cambridge alumni, by J. A. Venn, which seems to have eluded students of West's painting. Fellow Commoners were usually well-connected undergraduates who paid for the privilege of dining with the Fellows.

Among this pride of young lions, a special interest attaches to the one Virginian. The first Ralph Wormeley had died in 1651. Under the second Ralph, a secretary of Virginia who died in 1701, the family fortunes had reached their peak through the usual strategies of office, land acquisition, and marriage. The practice of sending the heir of Rosegill to be educated in England began with Ralph I's widow, Lady Chichele, who sent Ralph II to Oriel College, Oxford, in 1665, with the Middle Temple to follow. Ralph III and his brother John were wards of Robert "King" Carter, who worried about the possibility that sons of rich planters might be spoiled by "too long a taste of the town." "When I was in England," said he in 1705, "boys with the finest clothes and most money went away with the least learning in their heads." This would not be the fate of Ralph V, the cricketer, who would make his mark in life as a famous book collector, inspired, perhaps, by his memories of the college library at Trinity Hall, still today the best example of a medieval library in Cambridge. His appearance during his schooldays was preserved by no fewer than three fashionable artists: John Wollaston, who painted him in 1755 before he had left the colonies at the age of 10 for Eton College, and later, after he had entered Trinity Hall, by Robert Edge Pine and Benjamin West in the same year, 1763. No such pictorial record of his schooldays has survived for any other Virginia grandee.

The second puzzle about "The Cricketers," altogether more stubborn than the first, is the meaning of the setting. We see that it is pleasant, outdoor weather, with the sun shining through the clouds and the trees still in full leaf. The five students are certainly not dressed for playing cricket, like the

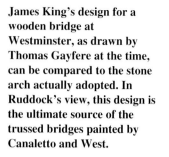

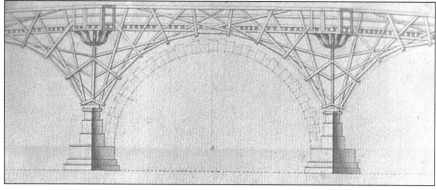

THE INSTITUTION OF CIVIL ENGINEERING, LONDON

players in Francis Hayman's picture, though two of them are leaning on cricket bats, and a third bat is lying at their feet. They are posing for a "conversation piece," dressed to the eyes, and too self-conscious to relax, unless the artist is not yet skillful enough to make them look completely at ease. Still it is a glorious moment that West, a fellow-American and no stranger to the ecstasies of the grand tour, wants us to feel as vividly as he did.

Behind James Allen and Ralph Wormeley, who are sharing the same chair, and Andrew Allen, whose hand is on Wormeley's shoulder, is a tall column of masonry overhung by a tree. Between Andrew Allen and Ralph Izard, the central figures, we catch a glimpse of two swans on a river behind them, before our view of the background is once again obstructed. Then comes a striking bridge of several arches with its balustrade sparkling in the sunlight. As four arches can be clearly counted between the center of the bridge and the southern bank, there may have been as many as eight arches in all. This is "the mystery bridge" to be identified.

It would be very unlike West not to have a rationale for this setting, which involved either his patron or his subjects or the game of cricket. There is nothing to suggest an English residence for Mr. Allen. If the column is more than an artist's prop, we do not know what it is. If such a bridge were near one of the famous London cricket grounds, like Molesey Hurst, Surrey, on the south bank of the Thames, where Garrick watched cricket, then the evidence has eluded us. The suggestion that the setting might have represented West's idea of Cambridge University is unconvincing. Only two of the students, Wormeley and Izard, were at Cambridge when the portrait was painted; the other three were in London. No bridge over the Cam would be as long as West's. If West had wanted to give them a Cambridge setting, the logical choice, which Pine was using in 1763 for his portrait of Wormeley, was a college background; and especially Trinity Hall, if that was the only college involved.

So we were driven back to the Thames. The modern catalog of West's paintings seemed to favor this option when it commented on a striking resemblance between West's bridge and the bridge at Walton-on-Thames, Surrey, as painted by Canaletto, the Venetian visitor, in 1754. Complete with the patron and his party (including his dog) in the foreground and his country

DULWICH PICTURE GALLERY, LONDON

Canaletto's "Old Walton Bridge over the Thames" was painted in London in 1754 for his patron Thomas Hollis, benefactor of Harvard College.

house on the hillside in the rear, this bridge is a stunning, soaring, airy structure of three arches, made wholly of wooden planks and ribs. However, the resemblance to West's seemingly solid bridge is anything but clear, and no reference is made to it in the second edition of the catalog, where only the Cambridge option is mentioned.

This author, in turn, was seduced by all the stir that the unfinished Blackfriar's Bridge was arousing while West was in Italy. Its architect, Robert Mylne, was just such another self-taught prodigy like West himself, whom he must certainly have heard about in Rome, where Mylne had preceded him. Mylne had returned from Rome in 1759 at the age of 26 and won the competition to select the architect out of 75 applicants, one of whom was Sir George Dance, father of Nathaniel Dance, the painter who introduced West in Italy to the art of conversation pieces. The controversy about Mylne's design was still the talk of the town when West got to England; and the Middle Temple, where three of his cricketers were living, was only a stone's throw from the northern end of the new bridge. Would this have influenced West?

But all the authorities turned me down. "Blackfriar's Bridge?" said one. "No, surely not! That was a stone bridge, not one with a wooden balustrade. My guess is that the bridge is not in London, but upriver, more like Marlow, for example." Another said, "Why not try your problem on Ted Ruddock, at the University of Edinburgh, who knows more about 18th-century bridges in Britain than anyone?" A phone call to this most obliging sage produced a promise, once he had studied a reproduction of the painting, to place West's bridge in the evolution of 18th-century bridges and to suggest where it might have been located.

Ted Ruddock has the knack of making hard questions sound easy. He ruled out the possibility that West might just have imagined his bridge on the ground that no artist could conceivably have invented some of its technical details; they must have been copied from life. Furthermore, as the type of framing used for the arches had only been known for about a decade in 1763, the bridge itself could be no older than that when painted. The technique used could be traced to the ferment of ideas and lobbying accompanying the planning of Westminster Bridge in 1738—London's first new bridge in more than 500 years. Its author was James King, who had submitted a design for a multi-arched wooden bridge that was not adopted for the Westminster Bridge and which was first used in 1750 by William Etheridge in his bridge at Walton-on-Thames. It became the prototype for several country bridges of which West's must have been one.

As explained by Ruddock, West's bridge was just as skeletal in structure as King intended or as Canaletto brilliantly depicted in the painting now at the Dulwich Gallery. He thinks that the approach arch at the extreme right, reddish brown in color, was probably brick, and that the remains of a former brick bridge may have been preserved at the foot of the piers, but feels quite sure that all five or six arches across the main channel were the trussed timbers on the lines of King's model. If the piers below the springing of the arches look like brick, that is probably an illusion; they are more likely to have been groups of timber piles covered with coarse, protective boards that turned brown after constant wetting. If the arches themselves, below the level of the roadway, seem to be made of radial blocks of stone, that is another illusion. He tells us that the parapet, which followed its own geometrical design, was typical of bridges at mid-century and often called "Chinese" in the pattern books.

West's travels in the fall of 1763, as indicated by his contemporary biographer, took him through a countryside richly furnished with private parks, princely patrons of the arts, and notable bridges. The royal family had its seats at Kew, Hampton Court, and Windsor, where new bridges had bloomed. The Dukes of Marlborough had built the longest span—over 100 feet—of any estate bridge in the south of England. The flamboyant ninth Earl of Pembroke, gentleman architect for the Westminster Bridge, was famous for his own bridge at Wilton.

It would have been no problem for West's young milords, who were supposed to be improving their minds as well as their taste in wine and women, to meet him anywhere he suggested in this sight-seeing. But just where to look, once we knew what to look for, was another matter. Two bridges in the Thames valley were considered by Ruddock, only to be rejected on technical grounds: the Kew bridge of 1759 and a bridge near Windsor in a print of the 1770s. He also had a final caveat: Was the river in West's painting broad enough for the Thames below Oxford? If not, upriver, or perhaps up a tributary, we must go. Though the Churchill motto "Never Despair" was very much in order, this half of the puzzle would not be solved as quickly as the other.

We may end this musing over West's masterpiece—as enchanting as many of his immense canvases are not—by reflecting that the American Revolution was only a dozen years away.

What would the future hold for the artist, whom we are leaving after little more than a year's residence in his mother country? He would be remembered as one of the great success stories of his age. National acclaim came in 1772 with his "The Death of General Wolfe." Appointed historical painter to the king, he was a close friend of George III until the sovereign's health failed. In 1792 he succeeded Sir Joshua Reynolds as president of the Royal Academy, earned higher fees than any English artist ever had, and was a venerated public figure in Europe as well as Britain. His studio in Newman Street was a mecca for American artists as long as he lived. When he died at the age of 82 in 1820, he was buried, predictably, in St. Paul's Cathedral.

Some critics had tried to bury him earlier. Hazlitt had called him "only a great painter by the acre." Lord Byron had sneered at "the flattering, feeble, dotard West, Europe's worst dauber and poor Britain's best." But secure in his own self-esteem, and always generous to others, West had gone about his work unmoved.

How had the five young friends, so buoyant and brilliant as "The Cricketers," survived the Revolution? Thomas Nelson of Yorktown, Hackney Academy, and Christ's College, Cambridge, who was a year or two ahead of them, is quoted as saying that of the nine or ten Virginians in England with him, he was the only one not to return a tory. It is impossible to check the accuracy of this judgment by a signer of the Declaration of Independence and wartime general of the Virginia militia, given the absence of records and the looseness of party labels, but it would be taken for granted that no family in the ruling class, like the Nelsons, Burwells, Grymeses, Randolphs, or Carters, was without its tories or loyalists.

Of the five cricketers, three came under surveillance or sanctions. Andrew Allen could not support the Declaration of Independence, joined the British Army, lost all his property, and moved to London. His younger brother James stayed out of politics, retired to the country when the war broke out, and died an unrepentant loyalist. Ralph Wormeley V and his father, surely of the same persuasion, died in their beds at Rosegill but only after giving security for their good behavior during the Yorktown campaign.

The other two cricketers, Ralph Izard and Arthur Middleton, joined Thomas Nelson on the patriotic side. Izard, perhaps the wealthiest of the five, chose to settle in England in 1771 but could not stay there after England declared war on the land of his birth. He moved to Paris in 1776, as an emissary of the American government, and eventually came home in 1779 to serve in the Continental Congress. Arthur Middleton declared himself early, signed the Declaration of Independence, served in the Continental Congress throughout the war, and spent the last year as a British prisoner in Florida.

This rupture in the political unity of the English-speaking people was an obvious setback to the future of cricket in the Western Hemisphere. While the music of bat and ball, British style, was being carried to every continent in the 19th century, an expanding United States was left groping for a summer sport equal to its manifest destiny. Happily another English game called "rounders," with roots as ancient and no social register to complicate its future in a democratic society, was ripe for improvement. The result was baseball.